PLAYING
FOR
KEEPS

*How a 21st century
businesswoman beat the boys.*

THERESE
ALLISON

Playing for Keeps

Published by:
Therese Allison
Huntington Beach, California
allisonpfk3@gmail.com
www.playingforkeeps21.org

Library of Congress Cataloging-in-Publication Data
(in progress)

ISBN-13: 978-1-7350886-0-0 Paperback
ISBN-13 978-1-7350886-3-1 Kindle

Printed in the United States of America

Book Design by www.KarrieRoss.com

First Edition: (September, 2020)
10 9 8 7 6 5 4 3 2 1

The book is a portrait of a successful businesswoman but also a love letter to Allison's family heritage.
~Matt Szabo, Los Angeles Times

She taught me a valuable lesson about gender equality long before I knew that gender equality was a thing.
~Jeff Eben, CEO, How Many Wins Foundation

DEDICATION

To my Dad,

Your example of being true to you, integrity and kindness have been a gift to me. Thank you for being my biggest cheerleader.

To Michael, Jamie and Tori,

Thank you for showing me what life is about.

Table of Contents

ACKNOWLEDGEMENTS

Thank you to Cara Badger Chase for being by my side for the last 50+ years. Your advice and unconditional support of me have meant more than you will ever know.

Thank you to my La Canada classmates Jeff Eben, Pete Magill and Bruce Craven. Your experience as authors helped me get to the goal line for this book. Thank you, Bill Prescott, for being my go-to for information on the La Canada High School class of 1979.

FOREWORD

by Jeff Eben

I am a competitor. As an athlete, survivor of a catastrophic injury, and successful educational leader, I have found my competitive spirit to be my most valuable asset. In fact, I thank God on a daily basis that I learned early if you are going to play, you should play to win.

I grew up on the mean playgrounds of La Canada Elementary School in the early 1970s. In this sleepy California village known for Hollywood executives and world class scientists, legends were being created every couple of hours on the kickball fields inside the fences of our little campus that remains famous to this day for its stellar academic achievement.

But those of us who were there during the days of Nixon, Flower Children, and Vietnam know the truth about our school: every recess was filled with drama and intrigue as a new kickball champion was crowned. I remember the greats: There was Big Matt, Paul, J. Dee, and Therese. That is no typo. Therese was the real deal. Smart, pretty, and ruthlessly quiet, she took her place alongside the boys and dominated us on a regular basis. In 1971, we probably were not fully woke, but we all wanted Therese Allison on our team.

Ok, so I exaggerate a little. Our playground was far from mean, and we were normal boys having fun at school. Therese, however, was not hyperbole. She was the first girl I ever saw who could compete with and beat the boys. She taught me a valuable lesson about gender equality long before I knew that gender equality was a thing.

She became a champion tennis player, but she was just as good in softball, bowling, and of course, kickball. I am not sure if kickball is an appropriate metaphor for life, but my early memories of her at recess turned out to be a pretty good piece of foreshadowing of her life as a mom and businesswoman. Simply put, Therese Allison has a special gift and a special story.

Playing for Keeps is not a simple autobiography.

It is the story of a woman who was born with a gift to compete and win on the athletic fields and the corporate boardrooms.

It is the story of a woman who channeled the energy of her ancestry and followed the lead of strong, courageous women who paved the way for her.

It is a beautiful love story about a woman and her father who shared a bond that remains strong after his passing through his art and writings.

Finally, it is a story about a woman who had her own Alchemist moment. After years of beating the boys in corporate offices around the world, Therese realized that the greatest victory of all was the ability to watch her children grow up and be a part of the memories they were creating.

I encourage you to immerse yourself in the Therese Allison experience. It is passionate and hopeful. It is a history lesson and a roadmap for anyone looking for perspective. It is the perfect elixir for the doubt that creeps into all of us when we face the daunting task of moving forward through the day-to-day obstacles that life throws our way. Always trust a kickball legend, and if you are stuck in any kind of funk, *Playing for Keeps* is your read.

~Jeff Eben
Author, Speaker, www.HowManyWins.com

Therese's Pearls of Wisdom

Over the years, I put together a list of the most important principles that paved the way for my success in my eighteen years of business. Throughout the book, I give examples of how they have been the framework of success, not only for me, but for my children and my family heritage over hundreds of years.

Be True to You.

People Do Business with People They Like.

I Can.

Pay Your Dues. Don't be entitled.

Luck is Where Preparation Meets Opportunity.

Where There is Chaos There is Opportunity.

Use a Velvet Glove (for women).

Always Dance with the Partner Who Brought You to the Dance.

Don't Talk Yourself Out of a Sale.

Treat Others the Way You Want to Be Treated.

Don't Leave Money on the Table.

Pigs Get Fat. Hogs Get Slaughtered.

Wear Your Selling Suit, and Check Your Shoes.

Always Take the High Road.

When you don't know the answer, say so.

Own up to your mistakes. Come up with a solution.

INTRODUCTION

If you take a healthy dose of Reese Witherspoon in *Legally Blonde*, add a cup of Sandra Bullock in *Miss Congeniality* and a tablespoon of Lucille Ball in *I Love Lucy*, I'm that girl. I'm the woman in a silk suit who tried to cram a case into the overhead while everyone in First Class stared. I thought they stared because I was late, but it turned out I had a rip in my skirt. I was the Lucy in pink pearls who turned into a warrior in the boardroom.

You could say that I got my big break from Hollywood… I was born there. I grew up in La Canada, a suburb of Los Angeles. People in La Canada were Hollywood creatives and rocket scientists. La Canada oozed wealth. The Allison family didn't fit into La Canada society. We didn't have the wealth, but we were creative and smart.

My father was an artist, a dreamer and the first love of my life. He painted beautiful canvases and created calendars showing the highlights of that month with color and flair. I still have those calendars and will share some of them here. Dad showed me how to create genuine connections with people, whether they were in the popular crowd, the wealthy *crème de la crème*, the barista at Starbucks or the guy next to us on the elevator. Like Rose on the *Titanic*, I could hang out in First Class or steerage, all the same to me.

As far back as I can remember, I wanted to win at everything. In my early years my energy went into sports, starting with playground kickball. That feeling of power when I beat the boys fed my incredible drive until I became a force of nature. In seventh grade I left-hand arm wrestled the strongest boy in junior high and won. My junior year, I was on the Varsity Tennis team that won the CIF Championship.

My dad used to tell people that I came out of the womb holding a tennis racket. I was voted most athletic and served as Associated Student Body president. My grades were also in the top 5 percent of my high school class.

That drive spurred me to the top of a male-dominated industry in the 1980s and '90s until I retired financially independent at the age of forty-three. I did it my way and stayed true to myself.

Shortly before my father passed away in 2015, I promised him that I would write a book about the Allison family's role in settling California. Ancestors of his mother, Lotta Snow, had crossed the Atlantic from Britain in the 1630s, ten years after the pilgrims landed in Plymouth.

My great-great-grandfather, Robert Allison, was business partners with California Governor Robert Waterman, an Illinois delegate to the first Republican Convention in 1856. The delegate who stood beside Robert Waterman was his friend, Abraham Lincoln. Robert Allison married Tempa Waterman, the governor's relative. My great grandmother was Mary Churchill of the Devonshire Churchills.

We are the story of crossing the plains in the Gold Rush of 1851, not to dig but to set up shops and provide goods to the miners. We are the story of helping Abraham Lincoln to the White House. We are the story of bringing water into California.

Just recently, I discovered the extent of my heritage. I never knew why I had such focus and that burning desire to win. My dad always said that I was like my grandfather, but I had never met Joseph Chester Allison (J.C.). He and Lotta both passed away by the time my dad was twelve. I was walking around with a blue-blood business pedigree and didn't have a clue.

My grandfather negotiated a treaty for an International Aqueduct with Mexico in 1932. He raced against William Mulholland to bring additional water from the Colorado River into Los Angeles. He paid his dues by eating, sleeping and studying the soil on the Colorado River in his 20's. He rose to the top engineering position by solving major flood problems on several occasions. Where there was chaos, he saw opportunity.

He worked with the Governor of Northern Baja for nine years in reference to the Colorado River, developing connections and cementing friendships. Chester and his lovely wife, Lotta, entertained dignitaries at their hilltop house in La Jolla. Don't underestimate the power of being liked. It is currency, making it one of the most important principles in business. People do business with people they like and trust.

When Los Angeles needed a bigger water source, J.C. Allison submitted a viable solution he had come up with years before. By 1932, his friend and colleague, the Former Governor of Northern Baja, was the soon-to-be President of Mexico. And there you have it, approval from Mexico. Luck is where preparation meets opportunity.

In 1936, the *Calexico Chronicle* printed, "Allison was one of those rare humans who combined the qualities of dreamer and practical businessman. He had the vision of the true pioneer, but he was also a skilled engineer and endowed with a high degree of common sense. He faced tremendous obstacles – and sometimes lost—but his optimism never faded."

I've lived by these principles all my life. They took me to the position of first female producing partner in a company with ties to Lloyd's of London. These principles helped me win again and again. When my son, Michael, wanted to go into business, I saw my opportunity to help him rise by coaching him in these same strategies. At the age of twenty-seven, he became one of the youngest Principals in a multi-billion prominent global company, headquartered in New York.

At the time, I had no idea that my ancestors had done the same for hundreds of years, stretching across the Atlantic to Sir Winston Churchill and Princess Diana. I had no idea that I had come full circle by representing women on the underwriting floor of Lloyd's of London after 300 years of male exclusivity.

I spent ten years in the insurance brokerage industry making my way to the top and another eight years working at that level. Along with my female colleagues of that era, we broke a lot of ground in the 1990s. Many women have made strides since then, but the gender landscape is still bleak in many industries. If you're a woman with that burning drive to beat the boys and climb to the top, this book is for you. Flex your bicep and get ready to arm wrestle. We still have a long way to go.

C H A P T E R   1

Fight Like a Girl

Keep calm and fight like a girl.[2] ~Anonymous

When I was growing up, a popular TV show had a tree clubhouse with a dilapidated sign tacked to the door that said, "No Girls Allowed." Even at age eight, that didn't seem right to me. I could beat the boys at sports, and they always picked me first when putting together a team. I was a winner, but I couldn't go in their clubhouse? Why not?

---

[1] Visit www.PlayingForKeeps21.org to view these images in full color.

[2] https://johnleskodotbiz.wordpress.com/2014/08/05/keep-calm-and-fight-like-a-girl/

When I entered the insurance brokerage industry, I was again on the outside looking in at an industry that was 95 percent male and still having two-martini lunches. I felt like my shoes were just inside the circus tent, watching others perform. I was twenty-six, blonde... oh, and I was a woman. Needless to say, I didn't fit in. I was just happy to be inside the tent. I didn't know it then, but the insurance brokerage industry would become my frontier. Twelve years later, I owned my share of the ring.

The Jonathan Club

In 1895, Los Angeles had two prestigious clubs: the Jonathan Club and the California Club. A local adage says the Jonathan Club is for people who run Los Angeles, while the California Club is for people who own Los Angeles.

The Jonathan Club started as a Political Club, then became a Social Club. Platinum Clubs of America ranks it as one of the top clubs in the world, and membership is by invitation only. Although the club was accused of racism and antisemitism in 1965, little changed. By 1975 women guests could enter, but they had to remain in certain areas. Not until 1987 did the Jonathan Club vote to admit African-Americans and women.[3]

Members of the Jonathan Club included President Ronald Reagan, Chief Justice Earl Warren, Peter O'Malley,[4] Henry Huntington[5] and Harry Chandler, publisher of the *L.A. Times* who owned the largest real estate empire in the United States.

At the age of eighteen, my grandfather, Joseph Chester (J.C.) Allison, met Harry Chandler who was thirty-eight years old. Harry Chandler put the capital S in Southern California as people wanted to say they were from Southern California instead

---

[3] https://www.latimes.com/archives/la-xpm-1987-04-25-mn-988-story.html
[4] owner and president of Los Angeles Dodgers
[5] railroad builder and land developer

of Los Angeles. Ultimately, J.C. Allison became Harry Chandler's "William Mulholland" in bringing irrigation to his land in Baja California. Without water, a piece of land in the desert does not have a chance to flourish. With water, it blooms like a rose.

In 1993, I met Mike Suter for lunch at the Jonathan Club where he was a member. We were with different companies, but sometimes worked together as I brokered employee benefits and Mike brokered medical malpractice. Mike is biracial, and I'm a woman. Only a few years before, neither one of us would have been allowed in that room.

As I was waiting for my salad, I looked around at the dark wood and old leather. I couldn't help but think that I wasn't the first Allison to conduct business there. I would find out that the Jonathan Club dining room was the very place where, eighty years later, my success story would intersect with my grandfather J.C. Allison's larger-than-life career. I earned my own seat in the club by my own hard work and strategy.

Prior to 1999 ACCOMMODATION OF DIVERSITY

"She's a woman.
How can she be worth it?"

Pay your dues.

In *Legally Blonde*, Reese Witherspoon plays Elle Woods in a classic trial scene where they are about to lose the case. Suddenly, something dawns on Elle that the male lawyers haven't figured out. The witness had her hair permed on the day of the murder, and her alibi said she was in the shower when the murder occurred. Elle knew the cardinal rule that after a perm you don't get your hair wet for 24 hours. She catches the witness off guard and wins the case.

Elle Woods was blonde, was dressed in pink and was totally underestimated. She never changed who she was to fit in. Her male colleagues soon learned she was exceptionally smart and a force to be reckoned with. I was that woman in my industry…except I changed my hair color along the way!

"She never changed who she was to fit in."

Working Upstream

While working at Corroon, I grew to understand the contracts and financing mechanisms between medical groups and the Health Maintenance Organizations (HMOs), and I developed a product called the "retention only" contract. This accomplished two things for my clients: saving cash flow and reducing administration fees. I sold the plan to Friendly Hills Medical Group.

Using Friendly Hills as an example, I approached the largest medical group, Mullikin Medical Centers, where John McDonald was my connection. John was known in the industry as the Godfather of Managed Care. After I became their broker, my book of business mushroomed.

Friendly Hills belonged to the Unified Medical Group Association (UMGA). Any Medical Group of any significance belonged to that association. I started specializing in Medical Groups placing benefits, and the UMGA became my major center of influence. I received referrals to all the CEO's in the industry simply by asking my clients' permission to use their name in a letter or a phone call. That one tactic opened doors at the highest levels.

This might seem lucky, but it was careful strategy.

Luck is where preparation meets opportunity.

Meanwhile, Frank McKenna and I frequently crossed paths because we had the same clients. We weren't competitors in the truest sense because we served our clients in different areas. For eighteen months, McKenna urged me to join him at Sullivan & Curtis. I wasn't interested. I had heard that Jim Kelly, one of the Sullivan partners, was verbally unkind to women. I figured I would get myself fired because, like my grandmother Lotta Snow, I wouldn't put up with it.

When Lotta saw a wrong, she spoke out. She was a brave woman for her era. In the late 1920s, my grandparents owned a hilltop estate looking down upon the La Jolla Beach and Tennis Club. The realtors in La Jolla had a gentlemen's agreement during that time that they would not sell homes to Jewish people. Despite this growing attitude in pre-WWII America, Lotta fought for membership rights for Jewish patrons.

She was also determined. Lotta had different views on politics from her husband, J.C. They would get into arguments outside their La Jolla home, and J.C. would end the fight by laughing and throwing Lotta into the fountain. She would not give in.

I also have a strong sense of fairness and how people are treated. I've been known to right wrongs when everyone else turns their head. I'm sure I get it from my grandmother, Lotta.

Be true to you.

Making the Move

During this time, I decided to try a new area of focus that put me in a position to go head to head with McKenna on an account. I won the business because I had established a good relationship with the CFO of that company, who was a woman. This was the first time McKenna had ever lost a sale on this line of coverage, and he wasn't happy.

I was new to the product and had to service this large account. Fulfillment would involve a learning curve. Now that I had caught the tiger, what would I do with it? At that point I realized that learning from McKenna would be a major asset to my career. We could lock up the medical group market by offering capitation stop-loss, employee benefits and medical malpractice (Sullivan's specialty) as one-stop shopping.

I called McKenna, raised the white flag and told him I was ready to talk about his offer of a position with his company. I'd join him, but only if I was promised a partnership position. I knew the salary-negotiation game had leveled up in my favor, so I tacked 50 percent onto my actual number. Since I had to be the one to throw out the first number, I wasn't going to leave anything on the table.

Don't leave money on the table.

McKenna went back to the partners and presented my number. Their response: "She's a woman. How can she be worth it?"

McKenna laughed and said, "She's worth it."

"She's a woman. How can she be worth it?"

Keep in mind, this was the 1990s. Sullivan & Curtis were old-school brokers associated with Lloyd's. Women weren't even in the business, let alone partners.

Ironically, John McDonald the Godfather of Managed Care told Jim Kelly, the very partner I had objected to, what a good move it was to hire me. The very man who had kept me from saying yes received that message from the most respected CEO in the industry. Can we say validation?

Frank McKenna was smart. He had spent a year and a half getting me on the hook, and he didn't want to lose me. He took a risk with his own income to sign me, a gamble that paid off.

Everyone in the industry knew that if Jerry Sullivan tapped you on the shoulder, you were a "made man" and on your way to becoming wealthy. In our case, Sullivan anointed McKenna. Then McKenna anointed me. McKenna was the partner who brought me to the dance, and I always dance with the partner who brought me to the dance.

Always dance with the partner who brought you
to the dance.

Shortly afterward, McKenna told me he was spinning off a division of Sullivan, and the principal producers would have an equity stake. First called Sullivan Kelly Managed Care, this company soon become McKenna & Associates.

The Other Shoe Drops

As soon as I gave notice to Corroon, I received a gag order. I couldn't talk to my clients for two weeks while they tried to convince my clients to stay with their company. Corroon did not know that McKenna shared a lot of the same clients. He worked for Sullivan, so Corroon could not gag him.

I was sweating bullets because my first-year guaranteed salary depended on moving my book of business to Sullivan. If clients did not move with me, I would have no income after a year. I thought it was worth the risk, and it was. Ninety percent of my business came with me in the first two months.

People do business with people they like.

———————————

I was honored to be the first female producing partner to buy into the Sullivan Companies.

The first couple of years, McKenna & Associates grew at a clip of 40 percent. During this time, MedPartners, an Alabama company, came into the California market and proceeded to buy up a significant percentage of the medical groups. The great thing about working in a niche industry is you can live big by specializing and having a good reputation. The not-so-great thing is you can quickly die if a company buys all the eggs in your basket. To keep this from happening we were always working our way upstream. Soon, we became the broker/consultant for all of MedPartners acquisitions across the country. I became the partner in charge of managing all lines. The MedPartners regime lasted several years.

"We were always working our way upstream."

The Buy-Out

In 1998, McKenna & Sullivan approached AON in Chicago, one of the largest brokers in the world, and entered into discussions about selling McKenna & Associates. This was the late '90s when the insurance industry was in acquisition and merger mania. Wall Street was rewarding companies that grew through acquisitions, thus creating economies of scale. The buying and selling of companies made some enterprising people very wealthy.

But when is enough, enough?

Prior to selling, John McDonald gave us sage advice after he sold Mullikin to MedPartners. He said, "Don't get greedy. Sell your business before the wave crests, so the buyers can make money and you have a win-win." We did.

Like my dad always said, "Just because you can, doesn't mean you should."

> When you've got a good thing and you get greedy, it always, always, always, always, always turns on you. ~Mark Cuban

> Pigs get fat. Hogs get slaughtered.

That year we closed the deal and sold our company to AON. As principals, they bought us out in stock. In addition, we all signed five-year contracts to head AON Healthcare Services.

At thirty-eight years old, I became financially independent. Not only had I broken through the glass ceiling of the Sullivan companies by being the first female producing partner, but in four generations of my California pioneer family, I was the first female Allison to break the glass ceiling of the Allison men.

AON bought our company for about $16 million ($26 Million in today's dollars). We decided to take our payout in the form of stock because the taxation is more favorable than cash. The downside of being bought out in stock is that if it is restricted (and ours was for a year), you have a small fortune sitting in one stock. If that stock becomes volatile, you can lose a substantial amount of money.

While I was a risk taker when it came to betting on myself, I was risk averse when it came to my buy-out. To mitigate the risk, I purchased a collar for my stock. This would limit my upside to 15 percent. In turn, my downside would have a floor of 75 percent. In effect, it imitates the benefits of diversifying the stock. This move was fortuitous because the stock went down to 50 percent of what was originally issued.

I spent the next five years as an Executive Vice President in AON's National Healthcare Practice. Toward the end of the contract, I met with the head of our region, Dennis Haney, to discuss what would happen when my contract was up. He said that I was one of the highest paid executives on the West Coast. I was making $1,170,000 in today's dollars. What he didn't know was that I was putting most of my salary in deferred compensation (to be paid out later) so that I could retire early. Like Elle Woods, I was doing it my way.

A LUCY MOMENT
The First Floor

My ancestors have been in California since the Gold Rush. That's 150 years of living in a mild climate. My first trip to Chicago was in January, and I didn't bring a coat. Worse, I wore some really nice Prada shoes, not knowing they would have salt on the ground. (Can you believe it!)

In the mid '90s, Caremark, one of the largest pharmacy benefit managers (PBM) in the country, decided to expand into the physician services industry, particularly Managed Care. Since Friendly Hills was one of the largest groups, Caremark bought them. Nothing like seeing your largest client vanish overnight.

Always working our way upstream, McKenna and I went to Chicago to pitch Caremark. It was do or die. We were either going to lose Friendly Hills or gain Caremark. If we landed the account, it would clearly be a marquee account for us, a career maker.

In the end, we won their business, mainly due to our expertise in risk shifting. At that meeting I met Marian Swanson. She had my number right away. With her deadpan sense of humor, I was perfect fodder for her. When I'd fly in for corporate meetings, we'd be in the elevator, and the doors would open. I would automatically get off, and the doors would close. I'd look behind me, no Marian.

Marian was on her way to the right floor. I invariably would show up 10 minutes later, and she would sit there smiling at me. It happened every time.

I worked with Marian for almost 10 years. Caremark continued to purchase medical groups around the country. As soon as they made an acquisition, Marian and I met with the physicians to talk about their benefits. Near Mesa, Arizona, the meeting became heated as the employed physicians waved their contracts, furiously announcing that their benefits could not be changed. Unfortunately, as soon as Caremark purchased the company their physicians' benefits became null and void. No one let the physicians know ahead of time. I was the messenger, and they wanted to shoot me.

A bunch of Wall Street types managed Caremark's parent company, MedPartners. They had assumed that if they got bigger, their employee benefits would cost less through economies of scale, otherwise known as volume discounts. However, that's not the case with benefits. So, MedPartners cut their budget by reducing benefits.

Many times, I would be the bearer of bad news. It wasn't fun, but it was my job.

Pay your dues.

After a horrendous day, Marian and I checked into a Ramada Inn Express. One of our offices had made the reservation. I got to my room, and it was icky. I took the sheet off of the bed to cover the couch because I didn't trust to sit on it. That night, outside noise and foot traffic kept me awake most of the night.

The next day, Marian agreed that the hotel was way too loud. When we arrived at the meeting place, the HR manager asked us where we'd stayed. When we told her, she got a look on her face and said, "You didn't stay on the first floor, did you?"

My eyes grew round as I nodded.

She said, "That place is known for truckers and hookers all hours of the night."

The joys of constant travel. Somehow, I was a magnet for these Lucy moments during my entire career.

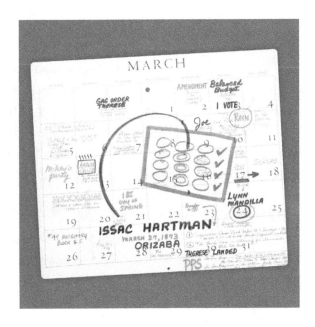

CHAPTER 2

Have a Career Plan

A goal without a plan is just a wish.[6] ~Antoine De
Saint-Exupery

Every step of the way, the most critical element is to plan
for success. Everything I did in high school helped get me into
college. Everything I did in college was to build my resumé to get
me a job when I graduated. Once I landed my first job, I learned
and observed and kept paying attention, so I'd be in the right
place for the next opportunity.

[6] https://www.goodreads.com/quotes/87476-a-goal-without-a-plan-is-just-a-wish

At 15½ years old, my first job was in a men's clothing retail shop called Chess King located in the Glendale Galleria. Buying a car was my first goal. No one can get ahead without wheels. By age 17, I got promoted to third-key manager which meant I could open and close the store and cash out the register. I saved up $600 and bought a yellow Datsun B210 from Lori Green's dad. Lori was a classmate at La Canada High School.

During that time, the Freeway Killer murdered twenty-one boys and young men and dumped them alongside freeways in Los Angeles and Orange Counties. I had to drive on three freeways to get to work. All the way, I'd peer over my white knuckles on the steering wheel, glancing at the sides of the freeway looking for bodies. On nights when I had to close the store, I'd race to the parking lot with my heart pounding. I worked at Chess King until graduation.

Although acceptance letters arrived from UCLA and Brigham Young University, I chose Cal Poly San Luis Obispo (SLO) and roomed with my best friend, Cara Badger Chase. Cara and I met on the curb when we were four years old, holding our blankies on the way to kindergarten. She's still my best friend today.

I chose Physical Education as my major because of my love for sports, with a minor in Corporate Fitness. I figured I'd probably end up as a PE teacher.

My parents helped me financially the first year, but after that I was on my own. I heard about a new restaurant named Spike's Place and got a job as a waitress, but I had my sights on a management position to add to my resumé.

In order to manage the restaurant, I had to work all positions. The cooks teased me mercilessly while I worked their stations. I learned to laugh at myself and go with the flow. This was the first time I realized that people like to work with people they like. Later, this transferred to: People do business with people they like.

People do business with people they like.

————————————

Since I always signed my tickets with my initials, the cooks started calling me TA. Eventually everyone else did, too. Spike's served forty beers from around the world. If you came in for a beer, you received a card with that beer number punched out. Once you drank all forty, you received a t-shirt and a plaque with your name on the wall. My claim to fame at Spike's Place was my plaque for drinking forty beers. It had my name as TA and hung right by the women's restroom. Spike's Place was a big party every weekend. It was a blast!

I went to college full time and managed the restaurant until I graduated. Not only did the position look great on my resumé, but I also learned about working with people, about organization and about finding solutions. Spike's gave me training in the trenches and laid a strong foundation for what came later.

Pay your dues. Don't be entitled.

————————————

Cara's uncle, Kent Badger, opened the way for my first job interview. He was the COO at Whittier Presbyterian Hospital, and they were looking for a salesperson for their wellness program. He heard I was in the job market, and bingo I had an interview.

Remember, hiring a referral is a win-win. You get a job, and the company brings in a vetted employee. My new position: salesperson in Whittier's new wellness program called Staywell. Since my minor was Corporate Fitness, the position was a good fit. This was the last interview of my life. I never had to apply for another job, because recruiters always approached me from that point on.

When looking for a job, go for the low hanging fruit first. People who know you might make a recommendation to someone who is hiring. Landing that first job through the low-hanging fruit approach was the springboard for the rest of my career.

"Landing that first job through the low hanging fruit approach was the springboard for the rest of my career."

In the 1980s, Corporate Fitness started taking off because healthcare premiums were increasing, making employee benefit plans too costly. Staywell operated under the premise that incentives for employees to adopt a healthy lifestyle would lower the company's healthcare premiums. They were the first company to offer a complete bundle for hospitals to sell as benefits packages.

I was their brand-new salesperson with zero experience for their brand-new product, never before offered in any market anywhere. I had no idea what I was getting into, but I was always up for the challenge.

After graduation, I flew into the Orange County airport to begin my new job. My co-workers, Joyce and Karen, were supposed to meet me at the gate to take me to the hospital and help me get oriented. They knew what I looked like, but I didn't know what they looked like.

No one met me at the gate. I stood in the walkway and waited for about 10 minutes. Finally, I walked back over to the gate.

I heard, "Therese," and turned around. Joyce and Karen had been in those seats the whole time, watching me. I thought, *They can't be that mean.*

That incident foreshadowed my experience at Whittier Presbyterian Hospital. The men didn't like me by the mere fact that I was a woman and I was smart. The older women didn't like me because I was young. Sometimes I could win them over, but sometimes not.

Shortly after I arrived, Whittier sent me to Minneapolis for their sales training. The Staywell program had a nurse teaching smoking cessation classes and a nutritionist who taught employees about healthy eating. Back at the hospital, I also became certified as a phlebotomist (a person who draws blood). Once I sold a program, I could draw blood and test for high risk factors, such as high cholesterol. I also taught the exercise portion of the program as aerobics classes.

Most sales in that department took eighteen months to close. After a year, Kathy, Joyce and Karen called me into a meeting and gave me the "Why haven't you sold anything yet?" dressing-down. As you can imagine, I felt ganged up on. I literally broke down and cried. I was all of twenty-five years old.

Soon after that, I started closing sales. One of my biggest accounts was the Whittier Union High School District. This client followed through with their wellness program and made a good case study. I sent a mailer to a list of insurance brokers citing Whittier as an example of their potential savings.

One of the brokers who responded was Frank Westin who worked for RKC & Co., a division of Corroon and Black. Westin offered me a sales position with RKC & Co. I figured, Why not? So, in 1986 I became an employee benefits insurance broker. Westin's specialty niche was school districts. I was like a sponge, going with him to meetings and learning as much as I could.

I built my business from scratch by cold calling to get appointments. During this time, a new section of the IRS code allowed companies to deduct medical premium contributions before withholding taxes. This would save money for both the employees and the company.

Knowing companies with more than 200 employees would have significant savings, I immediately acquired a prospect list of employers in that category. In addition to cold calling, I developed a flyer that was simply a case study telling how much Whittier Union High School District had saved. It included a return card saying, "For more information, call Therese Allison," and my phone number. I mailed the flyer to my hot list.

One of the returned cards came from Friendly Hills Medical Group, one of the largest Medical Groups in Southern California. I met their representative and showed them how our process could save them money. As a result, I replaced their broker of record who had worked with Friendly Hills for seventeen years. He had failed to present the new IRS code to them, and that opened the door for a young broker like me.

Luck is where preparation meets opportunity.

Over the next year, I learned the ins and outs of medical plan design and how to find the right placement with insurance carriers. I became more independent as my book started to grow. Threatened by my success, Frank Westin became jealous. I was still young in the business, but I knew his attitude wasn't right. I scheduled a meeting with the head of our division and told him what was going on. I asked if I could report to him directly instead of to Frank. Since my book of business was valuable to the company, he said yes.

This kind of move is risky. It can backfire on you, so you have to be sure you are of value to the company before taking this kind of action. Fortunately, it worked out for me that time.

Be true to you.

As time went on, my book of business grew larger. The more driven I became, the more rewarding my job became. When I scored a big account, I felt like I was back in high school winning the tennis championship. I always played for keeps, but this time I had a tangible reward. I absolutely loved it.

In these first years of my career, my plan was simple: to keep climbing. I had to take initiative and be smart about it. I had to play to win and be true to myself.

After five years with the RKC division of Corroon and Black, another division of Corroon called WF Corroon recruited me to come work for them, and I did.

This happened when the Managed Care industry was gaining popularity. The 1972 Knox Keene HMO Act allowed physicians and medical groups to receive a fixed fee per enrollee (a capitation) from insurance providers, whether that person received care or not. This shifted the risk to the provider. If a company had healthy employees, the provider enjoyed the profits. If the company had employees with heart attacks, transplants and other high-cost events, the provider had to take the loss.

After I saw how I'd nudged out the former broker with Friendly Hills, I was always on my toes to make sure I kept my clients informed of the latest types of coverage and the latest regulations. I was the person everyone asked, "So, what's new?" because I always had cutting-edge information. Also, I was always thinking outside the box, looking for a new perspective that could provide a solution for some stress point no one else was addressing.

"I was always looking for a new perspective that could solve a stress point no one else was addressing."

One day, the thought occurred to me that Friendly Hills was taking all of the physician and hospital risk for their HMO members because they owned a hospital. They were paying premiums as the insured and also providing the care. I thought Friendly Hills should be able to keep the capitation fees on their own employees.

The first call I made was to Frank McKenna at Sullivan and Curtis. Because we shared some of the same clients in a noncompetitive way, we often crossed paths at big events. An insurance broker, Sullivan and Curtis specialized in brokering coverage to hospitals and physicians. They had ties to Lloyd's of London. In the early 1980s, Frank McKenna developed a product through Lloyd's that would transfer the provider's risk above a certain threshold. This was known as the Capitation Stop - Loss contract.

I asked McKenna if Lloyd's would write an addendum stating that Friendly Hills' employees would be included in the capitation stop-loss policy. If he could make that happen, Friendly Hills would have a premium infinitely lower than traditional self-insured stop-loss. They would spread the risk across 500,000 employees vs. the regular stop-loss on 1,500 employees.

Once I got approval from Lloyd's through Frank, my next step was to meet with Friendly Hills' HMO, PacifiCare, and get them to sign off on the concept. Here are some steps that I took to increase my probability of convincing PacifiCare this new approach was a win-win for both companies. Covering all bases is essential when bringing this kind of innovation to the table.

Some guidelines when negotiating:

- Cover your bases – Know your product inside and out. Be the expert when you go into a negotiation, so you won't get caught off guard. Be quick on your feet.
- Know your leverage points –The more competition in your market, the more favorable the client's rate should be. Also, find areas where the client has

additional benefits from working with you, aside from cost. Show them how much they need you.

- Never throw out the first number – You might leave money on the table. If you do have to throw out the first number, make it a good one.
- State your case – In this meeting with Pacificare, I explained what I wanted to accomplish for them by breaking down their premium dollar. Then, I took away the cost of services they would no longer provide. Their first question was, "Will the plan have reinsurance?" and I replied, "Lloyd's has already signed off."
- Know what you are after – Memorize your lowest number and the number you'd like to have. For Friendly Hills, their administration fee was 1/3 of their current rate. They were also protected from catastrophic loss by Lloyd's of London with a minimal premium. Their payment fell within the range of my lowest and like-to-have numbers—so I was also happy with the deal.

This was the first time I thought about brokering capitation stop-loss. In order to enter this arena, I needed another carrier to come into the marketplace besides Lloyd's of London. McKenna had a corner on the Lloyd's market. When I entered capitation stop-loss, McKenna would become my competitor, so I couldn't keep using him as my Lloyd's contact.

Eventually, Anthem stepped up to the plate. I used Anthem to pitch the Pacific Physician Services account against McKenna and Lloyd's. And I won.

Like Elle Wood's, I had entered the "Harvard School of Insurance Brokerage."

1999 - 2003 LINK

"What do you want to be
when you grow up?"

THE ALLISON HERITAGE:

J.C. Allison Paid His Dues

On August 9, 1906, 300 million cubic feet of water flooded the Imperial Valley each hour, covering towns and farmland to create the Salton Sea. The flood conditions were so new, engineers could not agree on how to resolve it.

My grandfather, J.C. Allison, had arrived in the Imperial Valley in 1902 at the age of eighteen to join his father in a cattle camp on the Colorado River below the Mexican border. He ate and slept beside the Colorado River for several years and became familiar with the river and its soil.

When the Imperial Valley flooded, J.C. had already been on site for four years. He observed how some of the best civil engineers solved this flooding incident. He helped build the various solutions they came up with at the time. This was grueling work in difficult conditions, but J.C. loved it.

Pay your dues.

That was the beginning of J.C.'s career in engineering the Colorado River to irrigate the Imperial Valley and Baja California. During this time, he met Harry Chandler, soon-to-be publisher of the Los Angeles Times.

When Volcano Lake flooded from 1912 to 1915, J.C. was an engineer working on solutions, but the Volcano Lake situation wasn't fully resolved. When the Colorado River flooded the following year, J.C. got an idea that provided a solution for Volcano Lake.

Water was a frequent problem in those days, whether too much or not enough. During times of drought, he constructed hydraulic weirs across the Colorado River to bring water to needy areas. This chaos caused seasoned professionals to throw up their arms in frustration, but my grandfather saw opportunity.

Where there is chaos, there is opportunity.

Mentoring Michael

In 1998, my family had just moved into the house on the beach, when five-year-old Michael and I were playing garage hockey. As we were playing, I asked him, "What do you want to be when you grow up?"

He didn't hesitate. "A CEO," he said.

Unlikely for a woman in 1998, I would become his role model.

It is vitally important to have a plan in place as early as possible. If I had been content to be a waitress at Spike's Place, my resumé would have missed the word manager. Every decision I made in high school was to help me get into college. Everything I did in college was to build my resumé for a job when I graduated. I mentored my kids to do the same, and it paid off. Michael is a Principal of a prominent global company with headquarters in New York. Jamie has her Doctorate in Occupational Therapy, and Tori is on her way.

Here are two steps to get started early:

1. Find someone that you want to model yourself after and find out all you can about how they achieved their success. If you can't ask them, read everything you can and learn their story.

   Before I left for a trip to Chicago in 2008, Michael said, "Mom, will you write your story for me?" I said, "Sure." He was a junior in high school, and that was one of the smartest things he did. He knew that I wasn't the typical mom in business, and he wanted to know why.

2. When choosing high school activities for your children, look for a Model United Nations (MUN) or debate program and, if possible, have them go through all four years of the program.

   Michael participated in four years of Model United Nations in high school. It is an academic sport. He flourished and gained a tremendous amount of success and confidence. Michael and his three closest friends were the only students in their senior class who got into both Berkeley and UCLA. All four of them were high achievers in MUN. Jamie was also a high achiever in MUN. The MUN program may be the deciding factor in whether your child gets into the college of their choice or not.

When our conversations turned to college, Michael had a French-Canadian ice hockey coach who wanted him to go in the Juniors (precursor for NHL). Michael felt academics would take him further than sports, so he decided to go to UCLA. At the time, UCLA had an acceptance rate of 1 in 5 applicants. He also was accepted at Berkeley and NYU Stern School of Business. He became captain of the club hockey team, so he continued playing the sport during college.

LEFT: Michael and view from his office 2015—One World Trade Center in the distance RIGHT: Me and Michael 2018 BELOW RIGHT: "My job is done"

Every child is different. If you have a child who is an athlete and wants to play in college, playing at a high level can also garner a lot of attention when it comes time to put together a resumé for a career. In Jamie's case, she went to the World Championships of her sport, showing she has drive, discipline and perseverance. Almost every admissions officer or job recruiter wants to hear about that kind of experience. Anything that is out of the norm on a resumé is a beacon for conversation. It will melt the ice. People do business with people they like. People hire people they like.

Even after I grabbed the brass ring at age 38, I still had a plan. I wanted to retire early, and I set up my finances so I could. Today, my plan is to launch my youngest daughter who will graduate from high school in 2023. In the meantime, I'm writing this book and looking for my next frontier.

A LUCY MOMENT
The Ticket and the Cabbie

In the movie *The Proposal*, Sandra Bullock plays a high-powered editor who is constantly on the phone. While vacationing in Alaska, she runs outside to get a better signal, and the family's little fluffy white dog goes out with her. Gammy (played by Betty White) had just told Sandra not to let the dog out because the eagles will get him.

While Sandra is talking to an important client, an eagle scoops up the dog. Sandra chases the eagle, offering her phone in trade. She catches the dog, and the eagle goes away with the phone. Like Sandra Bullock, I was always preoccupied with work and stuff just happened. The Ticket and the Cabbie is a classic example of this.

McKenna and I were winding up a conference in Miami. Our next stop: London, to meet some CEOs for a meeting with Lloyd's underwriters. Back then, co-workers traveling with me knew they should watch me to make sure I didn't leave anything important behind. Apparently, McKenna missed that memo.

We arrived at the airport about two hours before our flight. I was on an important phone call when we got out of the cab, and the cab drove away. I walked a few steps, then turned around, "Where is my computer?"

My computer was still in the cab along with my first-class ticket to London. This was 1997, and I had to have my paper ticket. I decided to take a cab to the cab company and see what I could do to get my computer and ticket back. Frank stayed at the airport in case I needed to buy another ticket.

While I got into the nearest cab, he called the cab company. A few minutes later, I got a page with an address. Apparently, my cabbie was done for the day and had gone home. I showed the address to my cab driver, and he gave me a wide-eyed look. We couldn't have a conversation, because he didn't speak English. With a grimace, he put the car into gear with an attitude, and we set out.

I was clueless as to my surroundings. I just wanted my bag!

We pull up to a dilapidated apartment complex, and I got out greeted by barking dogs and screaming babies. I was suddenly glad I was wearing jeans and not my usual business attire. I walked upstairs and knocked on the door. The door opened with a chain still on it. A teenage boy peered through the crack.

"Is your father home?" I asked. "I'm here for my computer."

The boy shut the door, then opened it with the chain still on and passed my computer through. Everything was there. I give the kid $20. "Please tell your dad thank you for being honest."

Back at the airport, I was definitely a runner for the gate. Later, I found out that I had taken the scenic route to Little Havana in Miami. Tour guides tell tourists, "Don't sightsee in this high-crime area, or you will become one of the sights. You could be robbed or worse."

I wonder what the cabbie thought about the $20. I wonder if his son even gave it to him.

As with Sandra Bullock in *The Proposal*, everything works out eventually. Sometimes it just requires a small detour!

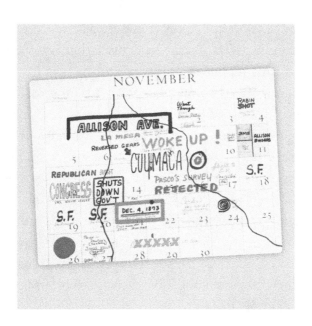

CHAPTER 3

Make Your Own Way

The pioneer spirit which founded America is a realistic insight into
how the impossible may become possible.[7]
~They Saw AMERICA Born

My father never had much. In his later years, he discovered that his great grandparents Robert Allison and Tempa Waterman became wealthy during the California Gold Rush. Dad's parents, J.C. and Lotta Snow Allison, had a sizable net worth as well.

---

[7] Dora Davis Farrington, M.A., *They Saw America Born*, (Pasadena, CA: The Davis-Allison Studies, 1941) http://homepages.rootsweb.com/~david-ca/america/america.htm

After J.C. died of a heart attack, a series of events took away the family assets. By the time my father was twelve years old, both of his parents were gone and he was left with very little. He grew up to be an artist with a strong dislike for big business.

My personality, on the other hand, was all about winning at any game I tried. I entered corporate settings with my eyes on the prize and never stopped until I reached the top.

I had no idea of the bigger picture of my history until I began researching to write this book. Now that I know where I came from, I can see the motivation and drive to succeed came from my DNA. However, my wins were all my own. When I stepped into the Jonathan Club, I was there on my own merits because I paid my dues and stayed prepared for every opportunity. I made my own way.

I Never Thought I Couldn't

From my first job at Chess King men's clothing store, my question has always been, "How do I get where I want to go from here?" The thought that something might be impossible never occurred to me. Early on, I also realized that going from Point A to Point B in my career meant working alongside people who had skills, relationships and experience that could help me on my way. I learned to spend time getting to know people and watching for opportunities to form strategic alliances.

People do business with people they like.

Alliances are far more than adding skillsets together. Two I-Can producers generate exponentially more together than simply adding their abilities. They create a synergistic Richter scale effect on the growth of a small company.

As I moved in the circles of my industry, I stayed alert for those synergistic relationships. This meant conversations over a glass of wine after a long day in a conference. It meant stopping in the hall to say hello, or striking up a conversation in a waiting room. It meant paying attention and taking names.

"I stayed alert for those synergistic relationships."

While at RKC & Co. I landed Friendly Hills Medical group and then California Primary Care Physicians in Los Angeles. That score brought me attention from Frank Westin's boss, Carl Ferrara.

A new winner on the team sparks curiosity, and the boss wanted to see what I was about. When I met Ferrara, he was over 50, and I was just over 25. Even more interesting for Ferrara, I was a young woman, which was unheard of in those days. By the time Westin started showing signs of jealousy, I already had Ferrara's respect. That's why I went over Westin's head and risked the conversation asking to report directly to Ferrara. I could have lost my job, but I received a yes.

I could produce.

I controlled my book of business.

I consistently made the company money.

Money earns respect. If your superiors know you can walk out and take your book of business with you, they will be more likely to accommodate your requests. The first language of anyone who's playing with the boys is the pocket book. I knew my power center, so forming strategic alliances happened quickly and easily for me.

"Money earns respect."

In the 1990s Rick Mayo recruited me from the Corroon and Black brokerage division to their consulting arm known as WF Corroon. I brought a substantial book of business with me.

This was important because the income I brought with me covered the company's expenses for having me on board.

I paid for myself.

Consulting companies in this arena didn't typically produce business. They provided expertise to service the accounts. They were not hunters. Because I brought my own book with me, I was again an anomaly because I brought income with me. Forming alliances with my managers happened easily for me because I made them look good to the higher ups.

When Frank McKenna and I first met, I was in my mid-twenties and Frank was around 30 years old. We were the up-and-coming generation. In the late '80s, we would see each other at the annual UMGA conferences. During break-out seminars, McKenna would speak about capitation stop-loss, and I would speak about employee benefits.

Pay your dues.

When McKenna created the first capitation stop-loss policy, he rose to the top of my list of people to know. He was no longer a peddler of coverage like thousands of others in his field. McKenna saw a need in the marketplace and created a solution. That put him in a class I called a visionary technical producer.

A few years later when I created the retention-only concept for Friendly Hills, I needed a connection with Lloyd's of London. Picking up the phone to call McKenna felt natural to me. I not only respected what he had created, I also respected his opinion. When my innovation for Friendly Hills became a success, he thought of me as a visionary technical producer. From that position, forming an official strategic alliance with Frank McKenna was only a matter of time.

Before you can form a strategic alliance, you have to know what you are worth, and what you clearly bring to the table. You have to know the strengths and weaknesses of your potential alliance partner. Choose carefully because strategic alliances can make or break you as you make your way to success.

"Before you can form a strategic alliance, you have to know what you are worth."

Don't Listen to Naysayers

Every step of my journey, I've made my own way and listened to my own gut. Not that I didn't consult with trusted advisers at times, but once I reached a decision, discussions were over. When I moved to McKenna & Associates, my guaranteed salary depended on moving my book of business. If clients did not move with me, I'd have no net to fall back on, and no corporate entity to fund my salary after a year.

I can.

Some of my friends and employees saw too much risk and tried to talk me out of going with McKenna. However, I was betting on myself. I knew I could deliver. I aimed high and refused the no.

If I had listened to the naysayers, I would have never retired at age forty-three. My children would have missed those years where they had my full attention, and I would have missed them.

Sometimes, you just know. And when you know, don't let anyone talk you out of it.

"Sometimes, you just know."

1987 CUYAMACA

"The Allison's weren't afraid of rolling up
their sleeves, of getting into the
trenches and making their own way."

THE ALLISON HERITAGE:

Gold vs. Cold Hard Cash

A pioneer is someone who forges new paths into previously uncharted territory. The Allison family is chock-full of pioneers. My dad and I were no different.

> *First, they ignore you, then they laugh at you, then*
> *they fight you, then you win.*[8]
> ~Mahatma Gandhi

Through his art, prayer pads and calendars, my dad pushed his limits and never encountered the impossible. Actually, what started out as impossible became his new normal. I saw this pattern more times than I can count.

Sitting in the office of Dad's cardiologist, we discussed my dad's pacemaker with a defibrillator. This combination unit would pace the rhythm of the heart. If the heart stopped, the defibrillator would shock the heart over and over until it started beating again, exactly like paddles at the hospital. If left switched on at the end of his life, the defibrillator would continue shocking, and he would experience a horrific passing.

With the defibrillator turned off, when the heart stops beating, the patient passes. Needless to say, my biggest fear was that my dad and I would pick the wrong time to turn it off. I couldn't bear the thought of him suffering during his final moments.

My dad always prayed that he would pass peacefully in his bed with his dog by his side. That morning, I went to his

---

[8] https://www.brainyquote.com/quotes/mahatma_gandhi_103630

condo and walked into his room. He looked like he was quietly sleeping with his dog wrapped around him. He showed no signs of struggle. His defibrillator did not fire. Yet, I had never turned it off.

My dad died exactly the way he wanted. While I was sad, I realized that what my dad had been saying all along was true, all things are possible with God.

Like my dad, I've always pushed my limits. Kickball, softball, volleyball, tennis—I loved them all. As I look back now, I succeeded because playing sports became my passion. I never thought I couldn't!

In 1978, the La Canada High School tennis team beat San Marino for the CIF Championship, and I had my first big win. Winning became my passion. I never thought I couldn't!

When I started my business, the strategy, the problem-solving, the deals, the wins, the people, the humor—they became my passion. I never thought I couldn't!

This was and is my normal.

"When I was passionate, I never thought I couldn't."

Over the years, people have asked me how I succeeded. My answer: explore what you are passionate about and push your limits as though the impossible is your new normal. Never think you can't.

This was the belief system of our pioneer ancestors who crossed the plains to make their own way. When they packed their covered wagons and loaded their saddlebags, they never thought they couldn't. They just did.

The Allison's were a true pioneer family in the old movie tradition, and their very colorful lives would make an entertaining novel. There is a great deal more which lack of space prevents us from including here…"[9]

Well, they were so right. We have continued to be a colorful and interesting family to this day.

Gold vs. Cold Hard Cash

In 1848, gold was discovered at Sutter's Mill in California. In 1851, at least four Allison brothers traveled from Iowa to California in ox-drawn wagons. My great, great grandfather Robert Allison and my great, great grandmother Tempa Waterman were among them. Tempa was a relative of Robert Waterman, the future Governor of California who became business partners with her husband, Robert Allison.

Governor Waterman CENTER: Nov. 25th, 1890   RIGHT: Robert Allison

Robert and Tempa made three crossings, traveling more than fifteen months in brutal conditions. Perseverance,

[9] "The Allison Family," *San Diego Families*, (San Diego Historical Society, circa 1930) This article was given to my father by the San Diego Historical Society in 2003.

courage, tenacity, strength—my ancestors had an undeniable conquering spirit.

I can.

Once Robert and Tempa arrived in California, they operated a hotel in Sacramento and sold supplies to the miners. Remember, 300,000 prospectors came to California during the Gold Rush. They mined $8.5 billion in today's dollars. Robert and Tempa knew that the wealth wasn't in the ground. The real money was in the miners.

Where there is chaos, there is opportunity.

The miners needed pickaxes, buckets, shovels, pans, boots, clothes, tents, mules and food. The demand was far greater than the supply, so, in the beginning a merchant could name any price. In 1848, a mining camp charged $100 for a pair of boots, $100 for one pound of coffee, $50 for a pickax and $16 for 2 bottles of juice. A tent went for $1 million in today's dollars, and a single egg cost $90.

The prospectors paid. They were mining millions. At today's values, an ounce of gold was worth $1,550. Everything was so expensive because the market could bear it.

The next smart move was to buy property, which Robert and Tempa did. In 1848, a city lot in San Francisco sold for $23,000. One year later, the same lot sold for $300,000 or the equivalent of $8 million today.

After the Gold Rush was finished, Robert and Tempa headed south to San Diego and purchased 11,000 acres of

Spanish Land Grants, including Rancho Cuyamaca and land from Augustin Olvera (Olvera Street). Robert's brother, Josiah Allison, stayed in the Sacramento area and started a famous rest stop called the Nut Tree. The famous story goes that he gave his niece Sally Fox a walnut. She buried it and it burgeoned into a huge walnut tree.

Robert and Tempa had a son, Joseph Augustus. When Joseph worked along the Colorado River, he brought his son, J.C., to work with him. The world was small back then. Governor Waterman took office in 1887. General Harrison Gray Otis became the President of the Times Mirror Corporation and publisher of the *L.A. Times* in 1886.

Harry Chandler married General Otis' daughter and that put him in line to become the publisher of the L.A. Times. In the European tradition, during those times people married for status or lineage or both. In the case of Joseph Augustus, it was both when he married my great grandmother Mary Churchill of the Sir Winston Churchill lineage. All of the Allison men married women whose ancestors migrated from England to the American Colonies in the 1630s.

The movers and shakers all knew each other. Governor Waterman and General Otis were both delegates at the 1860 Republican National Convention that essentially put Abraham Lincoln in the White House.

When the Gold Rush was over, California's population exploded as the California Dream was born. Seeing the trend, Robert and Tempa drove 600 cattle over the plains, their third time to cross the country. When young J.C. joined his father, Joseph Augustus, on the banks of the Colorado River, they were part of General Otis's cattle camp along the Mexican border. Otis, Waterman, and the Allison's were all cattle ranchers. Joseph

Augustus and his brothers also owned a butcher shop in San Diego where they took their cattle to the retail market.

Regardless of their wealth and social standing, the Allison's weren't afraid of rolling up their sleeves, of getting into the trenches and making their own way.

"The Allison's weren't afraid of rolling up their sleeves, of getting into the trenches and making their own way."

Mentoring Michael, Jamie and Tori

Live so that when your children think of fairness and integrity, they think of you. ~H. Jackson Brown Jr.

A few years ago, I encountered a father (an attorney and graduate of the University of California) who wrote a research paper for his daughter. My daughter was in the same honors program. It takes most students twenty hours to complete the same paper. Of course, word spread quickly.

This father had some convoluted idea that he was helping his daughter when he was actually sending her a message that she's not good enough. By his actions he told her, You can't do this on your own. With a collective sixty years of parenting under my belt, I can tell you that kind of message delivers a massive blow to a high schooler's self-esteem. The short-term gain of a good grade will never outweigh the long-term detriment of that father's message.

Let your kids feel the satisfaction of paying their dues, fighting their own battles and making their own way. Build their confidence with wins they have earned. Send your children into the world knowing they absolutely can. If you do, they will be unstoppable.

> **"Let your kids feel the satisfaction of paying their dues, fighting their own battles and making their own way."**

A LUCY MOMENT
When "I Can" Gets the Best of You!

Robin Williams and Jeff Daniels starred in a movie called *RV* where Jeff Daniels plays a dad who lives in his RV full time. During the movie, Jeff Daniels's character says, "RVs are fun. They're really not just for senior citizens. They're a great toy...but as soon as they leave the lot where you rent it, something goes wrong."

I couldn't agree more.

In 2014, I decided to rent an RV for a Utah vacation. Our destination: Zion. I brought along my friend, Cori Stockman, her niece Meghan, and my daughter Tori who was nine years old at the time. We also brought three female dogs.

We were a thirty-foot box on wheels filled with females. *No worries. I've got this.*

We set out early. The plan was to take the nine-hour drive to Zion where we'd meet Ken and Dorothy Walsh and their two daughters, Isabelle and Cassie. Ken and Dorothy have an RV as well, and Isabelle has been Tori's best friend since kindergarten. We were looking forward to a fabulous time together.

About 7½ hours after leaving Huntington Beach, we were driving in pitch dark coming down a hill in the Utah desert when the temperature gauge on the RV slid into the red zone. The last time that happened to me, I was in my Datsun B210.

Driving home from college, smoke started coming out of my engine. I broke down on the side of the road. It turned out that I had a problem with oil...I didn't have any! I never received the memo that you needed to put oil in your car.

My lingering PTSD from that experience forty years ago caused me to slow down and let the RV coast on the downhill grade, hoping we could make it to the town ahead.

By some miracle, we did make it. Along the way, the generator died. So did the lights and the air conditioner. Even at this hour, the outside temperature was 100 degrees. I parked on a side street and called the RV company. They told me they couldn't send anyone until the next day.

I decided to take matters into my own hands. I set out on foot to search for a gas station. I found one, but the mechanic was gone because it was late. I went into the store next door and asked the girl behind the counter, "Excuse me, do you know of a mechanic that can put some oil in my RV? It's just around the corner."

She had a bit of a drawl when she said, "Sure, let me call my boyfriend. He's a motorcycle mechanic." After calling him and speaking for a few seconds, she hung up and frowned. "Sorry. He's up in St. George for the night."

I said, "What town is this?"

She said "Paradise."

I started hearing the theme from *The Twilight Zone* in my head.

The door opened and two high school guys walked in. The attendant called their names and said, "Can you help this lady put some oil in her RV?"

Two minutes later, I walked out with them. They got into their dented truck and asked me if I wanted a ride.

I took a step back. "No thanks." I walked back to the RV. By the time I got there, they had their truck shining its headlights on the front of the RV with the RV hood open. After about 30 minutes, I realized they clearly didn't know what they were doing. I thanked them for their efforts and said goodbye. By this time, it was after 10 p.m.

I got back in the RV and noticed that the heat gauge had gone down. I called the RV company again and gave them an update. The friendly voice on the other end of the line told me I could drive the RV if the temp gauge stayed at the quarter mark or below.

I took a picture for proof, and we were on our way with the windows open to keep the air conditioner from overheating the engine. We went about four miles when we reached an uphill grade. After a couple of minutes, I noticed smoke was billowing up from Cori's legs in the passenger seat.

I swerved to the side of the road. "Everybody out!" I yelled.

Pandemonium followed with everyone grabbing purses, dogs and other valuables in a dash to clear the vehicle. Someone started crying.

We stood there for fifteen minutes until I was finally satisfied that the engine wasn't on fire. We got back in. I called the RV company again. They confirmed that a tow truck would arrive in the morning. I think it is safe to say that my pioneer ancestors would be appalled at this point!

We ended up sleeping in the RV where it stood by the side of the road. Open windows let in all the night sounds. Cowboys passed us in their roaring trucks, honking and yelling. Hot and miserable, no one slept.

Around 9 a.m. a big red tow truck arrived. The driver invited us inside his air-conditioned cab, and soon we were on our way back to St. George where we started from. He dropped us off in the repair shop's parking lot. Because it was Sunday, the shop was closed. We'd have to wait until the following day to get back on the road. At least we could plug the RV into an outlet there and have air conditioning. We had food and propane for the stove, so we settled in, enjoying the A/C, walking around the small town and taking naps.

The next day the mechanic had us back on the road in short order. We rented a car to have back-up transportation in case something else happened. Mila and I would take the RV, while everyone else would drive to the campsite in the car.

After they left, I drove to a shopping center. I picked up some snacks and searched for some wine. Finally, I asked the attendant for help.

He looked surprised. "Ma'am, we don't have any wine."

That's right. I'm in Utah. Ok, fine. All I wanted was get the hell out of Dodge!!

After about twenty minutes on the road, the generator stopped working again. Mila was panting, and I was melting, but we finally made it to Zion. Later, I learned the rental company had failed to tell me an important fact. When the gas tank went below a quarter tank, the generator shut down to save gas.

The moral of the story: Check your gas. Oh, and if you're in Utah and you want some wine, *fuhgeddaboudit!*

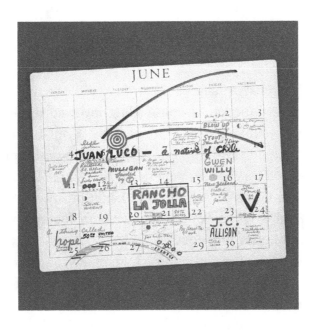

CHAPTER 4

Pay Your Dues

The elevator to success is out of order. You'll have to use the stairs…one step at a time.[10] ~Joe Girard

The universal metaphor for paying your dues is cold calling as a salesperson. When RKC & Co. hired me, they told me I needed to build my book of business. I would buy a list of companies and call each one to speak with the head of human resources. Their statistics said that one hundred calls would put

---

[10] https://www.goodreads.com/quotes/26980-the-elevator-to-success-is-out-of-order-you-ll-have

me in touch with ten people who would at least listen. Of those ten, I might get one meeting. What a depressing way to build a book of business.

The statistics handed down by the company seemed to imply that any success at cold calling involved dumb luck. I don't believe in dumb luck. I brought my "I Can" attitude to the game and stayed on the phone. Going through the process, I took notes and watched for patterns. Before long, I found a niche which opened doors faster and with better prospects.

"Find a niche which opens doors faster and with better prospects."

Preparation means putting in the time and effort to learn the finer points of the game. It means absorbing all you can about the bigger picture in order to recognize career-making opportunities when they appear and come up with a strategy to take advantage of those opportunities. Most anyone in business has heard of *Outliers: The Story of Success* by Malcolm Gladwell[11]. To paraphrase, Gladwell says that an expert, regardless of the topic, has invested 10,000 hours into mastering his craft or skill.

Luck is where preparation meets opportunity.

When you pay your dues in business, you equip yourself to clear the obstacles that come your way and open the path to success. This means running through every possible setback, objection and random happening, then creating a plan to control the uncontrollable.

---

[11] Malcolm Gladwell, *Outliers: The Story of Success*, (Little, Brown and Company, November 18, 2008) https://www.amazon.com/Outliers-Story-Success-Malcolm-Gladwell-ebook/dp/B001ANYDAO

People are always asking me about the secrets and tricks I use to get results. Sorry if this disappoints you: There are no secrets. There are no tricks.

Ask yourself where you are now, and where you want to be instead. Ask yourself what you're willing to do to get there. Then make a plan to get there. There are no shortcuts. Champions get into the Zone, shut out everything else, and control the uncontrollable.[12]

~From Tim Grover who trained Michael
Jordan, Dwayne Wade and Kobe Bryant

After entering the insurance industry, I spent five years putting in 10,000 hours. With this level of mastery, whenever I became aware of an opportunity, I would research my subject and figure out the field of competition. As soon as I focused on closing the deal, I had tunnel vision. No one could stop me. This is one of the reasons I have been so successful.

When the Caremark Rx opportunity came my way, I was ready. Caremark Rx had 13,000 employees. In the industry, we called companies of this size a marquee account, a career maker. We were a boutique firm and landing Caremark Rx would launch me into the category of handling jumbo accounts. I would have a seat at the pro table and play for higher stakes.

My main competition was Hewitt. One of the nation's top consulting companies in the benefits sector, Hewitt was the Health and Welfare consultant for Caremark Rx. Once Caremarkacquired Friendly Hills, Hewitt wanted to take over the Friendly Hills acquisition. Caremark Rx also happened to be

---

[12] Tim S. Grover, *Relentless: From Good to Great to Unstoppable* (New York, NY: Scribner, March 11, 2014), p 51. https://www.amazon.com/Relentless-Unstoppable-Tim-S-Grover/dp/1476714207

headquartered in Hewitt's backyard in Chicago. We were David, they were Goliath. McKenna and I had our work cut out for us, but we knew that sometimes being a David has its advantages.

> *Looking at David and Goliath in business, most people fail to recognize the advantages an underdog brand has when facing off against a competitor who has strength, size and wealth. And that's exactly why nimble, upstart companies often beat Goliaths.*[13]

~Malcolm Gladwell

The difference between our company and our jumbo competitors: We were a California broker, and I had personally created the retention product for Friendly Hills Medical Group. This proved my intimate knowledge of the managed care physician market. Caremark Rx was acquiring physician groups in the managed care market. I saw a perfect fit. Now, to convince Caremark Rx to see things my way.

At the beginning, McKenna and I had made plans to work our way upstream. We knew the key to getting business would be how well we differentiated ourselves. My retention concept and McKenna's capitation stop-loss with Lloyd's had worked well for us separately. When combined, they had a Richter scale effect. For Caremark Rx, we sweetened the deal with the ability to deliver more lucrative terms for their physician's long-term disability.

In our case, we were a niche player with creative solutions. Producing creative solutions was the chink in Hewitt's armor.

Our careful strategy locked Hewitt out. While Hewitt continued to provide administrative services for their own benefits, McKenna & Associates became the broker for all the

---

[13] Malcolm Gladwell, *David and Goliath: Underdogs, Misfits, and the Art of Battling Giants*, (Little, Brown and Company, October 1, 2013). https://www.amazon.com/David-Goliath-Underdogs-Misfits-Battling/dp/0316204374

medical groups Caremark Rx acquired. If you set yourself apart when going after business, you create an uneven playing field to close a deal.

"If you set yourself apart, you create an uneven playing field to close a deal."

In landing this account, several principles came into play:

- Pay your dues—I had put in my 10,000 hours and worked hard to stay knowledgeable and current in a constantly changing industry.
- I Can—I had the chutzpa to go after this whale named Caremark Rx.
- Where there is chaos, there is opportunity—Mergers are messy and I had proven my ability to clean up a mess.
- Luck is where preparation meets opportunity—Staying on top of the markets, the regulations, and the relationships put me in the sweet spot to be the favored choice (despite my female gender).
- People do business with people they like—If you have a competitive product, winning the game becomes all about relationships. I had worked with, dined with and hung out with many people involved in the process. Whether in 5-star restaurants or a dive bar after a conference, I felt comfortable anywhere and with pretty much anyone. And, just as important, they felt comfortable with me.

"If you have a competitive product, winning the game becomes all about relationships."

All of these came together in a massive play and we landed this marquee account that helped make my career.

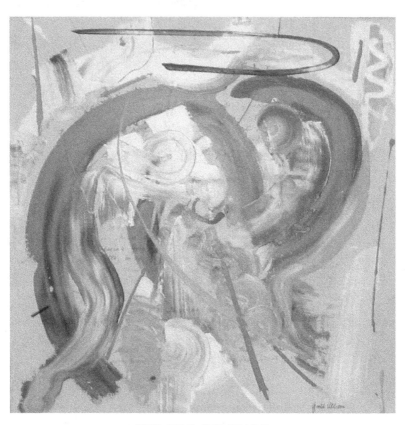

2003-2015 COLORADO

"Arguably, no watercourse in the world is more fought over or sustains more human life and economy than the West's greatest river, the Colorado."

Allison vs. Mulholland—
The Race for L.A. Water

Named after William Mulholland, one of the famous civil engineers of the early 1900s, Mulholland Drive was legendary for street racing in the 1960s. This road has been featured in a significant number of movies, songs and novels. You can almost feel the history of Hollywood while driving on it—the midnight gatherings, the flirting with death, the smell of fame and fortune wafting from the Hollywood hills.

In the 1930s, a different kind of race took place between William Mulholland and my grandfather, J.C. Allison. The stakes were high. The winner would forever be known as the pioneer engineer responsible for bringing water from the Colorado River into Los Angeles. Nearly a century later, Los Angeles would become the fifth largest economy in the world and Mulholland Drive would become world famous.

My father loved to clip articles and make notes on them. I found the article below in his files. Although the article was written in 1944, it referenced an interview with J.C. in 1916 when he was thirty-two years old. Fifteen years before he entered the Los Angeles water race against Mulholland, J.C. said:

Someday, this great Imperial area will be protected against flood and drought by the construction of a great dam far up the river in the Grand Canyon region. When that day comes, the Colorado river will become nothing more nor less than a big irrigation canal into which water will be turned from the dam reservoir as it is needed.

Then there will be plenty of water for every acre of

land in the Imperial basin and the delta region...with no fear of such a flood as swept down across the basin in 1905 and 1906.

This is a quotation from one of the most interesting interviews I have ever had in my experience as a newspaperman. The words were spoken by Chester Allison over 28 years ago, as I stood with him on Black Butte and looked northward over the American and Mexican Imperial valleys.[14]

~R.H. *Calexico Chronicle*

Most people have heard about the Los Angeles Aqueduct built in 1913, as it was the basis for the movie, Chinatown. Until now, few have heard my grandfather's story about his proposed International Aqueduct to bring water from the Colorado River into Los Angeles in 1932. My grandfather's story is a lost chapter in the epic saga of California water.

In his book, *The State of Water*, Obi Kaufman explores the past, present and future of water in California. He summarizes the battle over the Colorado River: "Arguably, no watercourse in the world is more fought over or sustains more human life and economy than the West's greatest river, the Colorado."[15]

When J.C. Allison was forty-eight years old, he entered in a competition with William Mulholland who was famous in that time for heading the Parker Dam project. My grandfather had years of experience and friends in high places. What he didn't have was the lead role in big projects like Mulholland. My grandfather was David, and Mulholland was Goliath.

---

[14] R.H., *Calexico Chronicle*. No other information available. The italicized quote was from 1916, and the full article was written circa 1944.

[15] Obi Kaufman, *The State of Water: Understanding California's Most Precious Resource*, (East Peoria, IL: Heyday, 2019), pp 103,104.
https://www.amazon.com/State-Water-Understanding-Californias-Precious-ebook/dp/B07NC9CJMG

"My grandfather was David, and Mulholland was Goliath."

Like a military general, my grandfather mapped out a careful strategy in his war room with his compatriots. He felt Mexico held the key to victory.

Where there is chaos, there is opportunity.

———————————

J.C. spent most of his life studying the Colorado River, both in the United States and Mexico. When he was young, he would eat and sleep on the Colorado River for days. He worked on the Colorado River in conjunction with the Governor of Northern Baja for nine years. As a result, he was aware of the Laguna Salada reservoir in lower California and Mexico.

The Laguna Salada is a vast reservoir 20 miles below the U.S.-Mexico border. In those days, it was thought to be the largest natural reservoir in the world. The Laguna Salada, "salty lagoon" in Spanish, is 33 feet below sea level and sprawls over 160 miles of shoreline. It is 37 miles in length and 11 miles at the narrowest place.

Pay your dues.

———————————

J.C.'s plan to access the Laguna Salada had a large advantage over the Parker Dam Route. Positioned farther down the Colorado River, his planned aqueduct would catch the Gila River near the Mexican border and deliver twice as much water to Los Angeles and the Coastal plains. Mulholland's plan couldn't match this amount of water delivery.

J.C. was so far ahead of his time, his fellow engineers saw his idea as a joke—until the Hoover Dam became a fact. This

San Diego Herald clipping[16] gives the details of the Allison-Forward plan, J.C.'s brainchild.

1932 ALLISON-FORWARD COLORADO RIVER PLAN

The advent of the Hoover Dam piqued J.C.'s curiosity. He pulled out all of his old surveys about water going from the Hoover Dam to the Gulf of California. His surveys showed that the project was completely feasible.

---

[16] A. R. Sauer, "Allison-Forward Colorado River Plan To Put $50,000,000 At Work in County of San Diego," *San Diego Herald*, February 11, 1932, front page.

In 1931, he used tens of thousands of his own money and, since the Colorado River crossed the border, took on the task of convincing the Mexican government to enter into a treaty. For the plan to work, an International Treaty with Mexico had to protect the United States "from any aggression through which the canals of the Allison-Forward project, or International Project, as it is generally known, would go in Mexico."[17]

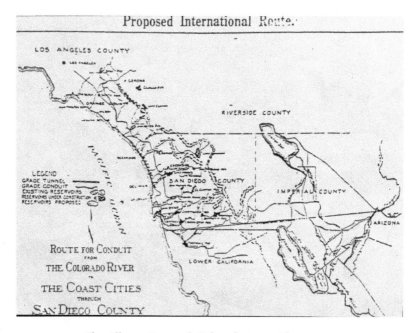

The Allison-Forward Colorado River Plan Route

He didn't let a little thing like negotiations with a foreign government stop him. Why not? Because his old friend, the former Governor of Northern Baja, was the soon-to-be President of Mexico. His relationships paved the way.

---

[17] Ibid.

People do business with people they like.

Like his ancestor, John Churchill (the 1st Duke of Marlborough), J.C. Allison was the front man for the project. Not only because the plan was his brainchild, but also because he had mastered the arts of diplomacy and persuasion. He had paid his dues

.

Pay your dues.

J.C. went head to head with Mulholland during the Great Depression. J.C.'s personal investment of $30,000 would be $528,029 in today's dollars. He felt the risk was worth it because he was absolutely certain his plan would work. The cost for the Allison-Forward plan was projected at $203 million, or $3.6 billion in today's dollars. That would be daunting to most people, even seasoned businessmen. J.C.'s "I Can" spirit kept him moving forward. He had confidence because he knew what he was doing.

J.C. came from a strong heritage. The California pioneer settlers from his father's side of the family combined with his mother, Mary Churchill, who was from the same lineage as Sir Winston Churchill. J.C. had iron resolve in his blood. He knew his own value and the value of his experience. J.C. was the game changer that was going to bring the Churchill's to Chinatown.

Mentoring Tori and Jamie

"Champions don't become champions when they win the event, but in the hours, weeks, months and years they spend preparing for it. The victorious performance itself is merely the demonstration of their championship character." ~ T. Alan Armstrong[18]

My girls, Tori and Jamie, are both driven. Still in high school, Tori does her own work and earned a 4.4 GPA, ranking 3rd out of 738 freshmen in the Class of 2023. I never have to ask her if she has done her homework. She earned her way into varsity volleyball as a freshman with a starting position as a sophomore. She pays her dues, and she makes her own way.

Like her ancestors before her, Tori has the undeniable conquering spirit of a pioneer.

Jamie went to the World Championships of her sport for the same reason: she earned it. She is also earning her Doctorate, both scholastically and financially. She pays her own way.

There are no shortcuts. Like my son, my daughters are in training to win at the game of life—and they are already winners.

---

[18] https://www.goodreads.com/quotes/145082-champions-do-not-become-champions-when-they-win-the-event

A LUCY MOMENT
First Class Entertainment

In *Miss Congeniality*, Sandra Bullock plays an FBI agent who is a boot-wearing, jeans-loving tomboy. In the movie, she goes undercover, and her team spends days transforming her into a beauty contestant. When she walks from the hanger to the private jet, she looks amazing.

Elegant steps to the music of "Mustang Sally," hair blowing in the wind, she's got the attitude of a winner...until she trips over her own foot and takes a header onto the asphalt.

I'm that girl.

Airports were my kryptonite. I was always running late with my head focused on work, and stuff just happened. Marian, my elevator "friend," was with me one time when we were leaving via O'Hare to go to Birmingham, Alabama. We went through security and arrived at our gate just in time.

I looked in my bag, and I couldn't find my calendar. Back in the 1990s, that paper calendar was my life. I had no choice but to run back to security.

Sure enough, I had left my planner in the bin. I grabbed it and dashed back to the gate just before they shut the door. In First Class, I lifted my carryon bag to put it into the overhead. It didn't fit. I shoved as hard as I could. No good. I glanced around to see a dozen men in suits staring at me.

Marian had her head down and her hand over her eyes. Her shoulders were shaking a little.

I decided to take some stuff out of my case, so it would fit in the overhead.

Unzipping the top, I dug inside to find something solid to pull out. The first thing my hand touched was a square plastic bag. I pulled it to the surface, triumphant...for about three seconds.

While packing that morning, I had searched everywhere to find a bag for my Velcro curlers. Finally, I came across an empty plastic Kotex® bag that was the exact size I needed. It even had a drawstring. Perfect.

Suddenly I had the feeling of being in the checkout line when the cashier calls, "Price Check!" and waves around the most embarrassing item you've purchased in months.

Gripping the plastic, I hesitated. I could either gate-check the bag or take that plastic Kotex® bag out of my case in full view of my audience.

I took it out.

What seemed like hours later, I sank into my seat, out of breath, sweating and flustered, with a feeling that my hair looked like a steel wool pad. I shoved that plastic bag under the seat in front of me and kept it pinned under my shoe.

Marian kept smiling. Come to think of it, she smiled that entire trip.

CHAPTER 5

Be Yourself

This above all: to thine own self be true, and it must follow as the night the day, Thou can'st be false to any man.[19] ~Shakespeare, Hamlet

In 1976 when I was 15, my big sister Gigi committed suicide. She was 21. When we got the news, my world became surreal and strangely foreign. The pain took my breath away, and I don't remember breathing again for years. I had lost my big sister.

[19] William Shakespeare, *Hamlet*, Act 1, Scene 3

If losing Gigi weren't horrific enough, in that split second, I went from being a regular kid at school to becoming the sophomore whose sister took her own life. Wherever I went, secretive glances and whispers followed me like a wake follows a ship. Friends avoided me, not knowing what to say. I had won the lottery of despair without ever buying a ticket.

Somehow, I had to figure out how to work through something so unspeakably horrible that no one wants to talk about it. I also had to confront the question that haunted me: "Is suicide going to get me, too?"

When I landed my first job at 15½, the raw agony of losing Gigi changed my perspective about the future. From that point on, I was on a mission to get far away from that awful day when she died. I pushed forward in my career not only for myself, but for her…for the future she would never have. The words on Gigi's memorial, "To Thine Own Self Be True," fueled my drive and powered my resolve.

"I pushed forward in my career not only for myself, but for Gigi."

Twenty-eight years later, in 2004, my dad had an open house in La Canada. One of the guests asked me if I was Gigi's little sister, and I said yes. We went into another room to talk more privately.

"How has your life been?" she asked.

I gave her a quick overview: three beautiful kids, great career and my early retirement that same year.

She said, "You were the light of Gigi's life. She always hurried home from school to take care of you."

My eyes started burning. "She called me her Tweety Bird," I whispered.

"She is your Guardian Angel," the woman said.

"She is your Guardian Angel."

Something inside told me the woman was right. All of my life, there could be chaos around me, but I would come out smelling like a rose. Whenever I had a big win, everyone always joked that I had a Guardian Angel. Gigi was the wind beneath my wings.

That day in 1976 was one of those before-and-after moments in our lives. Before, I considered us a normal family. After, my mother was never the same. The house felt quiet and lonely, as though someone had vacuumed out the air.

Dad and I started hanging out together for comfort and company. We became close.

My dad was a what-you-see-is-what-you-get kind of person. So am I. When I was first in business, I thought I had to act more mature and look smart. Soon, I realized that people responded better to me when they knew I was authentic. I was smart. I was funny. I was silly. I was honest. I was me.

Dad was the quintessential example of being true to yourself.

Be true to you.

My dad was an artist who sold carpet for a living while raising his family in the beautiful, wealthy suburb of La Canada Flintridge. During McGovern's 1972 Presidential campaign, my dad was listed among fifteen registered Democrats in a city of 25,000 Republicans. He lived in that area for forty-seven years. Known for his activism in holding back big developers, he was a worthy adversary who used charm to disarm his opponents.

"Dad was a worthy adversary who used charm to disarm his opponents."

A few years before he passed, he told me of his younger days in La Canada, back in the early 1960s. He had lost his job at Bullock's in Pasadena while he had a mortgage, a wife and three girls to take care of. Without missing a beat, he washed dishes for Delrod's restaurant in town and did odd jobs for some of the La Canada residents. I was amazed by his courage. He did whatever he needed to do to keep a roof over our heads.

After Gigi left us, Dad started painting abstracts. Painting helped him express his feelings.

He had always been a tad different from the norm. He loved it when someone would say he was crazy. "I wouldn't have it any other way," he'd say as though it were a wonderful joke. In his later years, post-it notes with scrawled inspiration covered his kitchen cabinets. His wall calendars seemed as though *A Beautiful Mind* and Picasso collided causing an explosion of bold colors.

"Dad loved it when someone would say he was crazy."

He loved to talk. Whenever he called, I knew if I picked up, we would be on the phone for 45 minutes, and he'd do most of the talking!

My nephew, Justin, tells the story about Dad at the gas pump. He never learned that the pump had a little lever to keep the pump running when you take your hand off. Every time he filled up, he would stand and hold the handle.

One time we were together, and I was the one pumping gas. I set the handle and pulled the window squeegee from the holder to wash my windshield. Dad yelled at me, "How are you walking away and it's still pumping?" I tried to explain it, but he couldn't seem to get it and kept holding the handle as usual.

He was also clueless when it came to coffee cup lids. So many times, I've seen him struggling to drive while removing the lid from his coffee cup, often spilling hot coffee over himself and the car, almost hitting the guard rail and swerving back. This was the chaos that seemed to follow him.

One day I asked him, "Why aren't you drinking from the hole in the lid?"

He retorted, "Because I don't have a straw."

That was my dad's charm. I have to admit, I didn't fall far from the tree! I'd be the one knocking the toothpicks off the counter, but as soon as they hit the floor, like Rain Man, I could give you the count. That was me in business.

Employees would come into my office with a business problem they couldn't figure out. In minutes, I would come up with a solution. As they were walking out, I would think, *Why didn't they see that?* This happened a lot.

One morning, I came across one of Dad's notes that read: "It takes tremendous courage to be yourself." I realize now that by being himself he gave us the best gift of all. If you can just be who you are in business, you will go a long way. People will trust you more.

"It takes tremendous courage to be yourself."

1934 From left, President of Mexico - Abelardo Rodriguez, unknown cabinet member, Frank Fletcher, J.C. Allison. At Chapultepec Castle, Presidential Residence, Mexico City.

"I will try and reach home before Christmas but must come immediately back here for… the water business of the next International Aqueduct."

The Race Continues—J.C. and the President of Mexico

In 1920, Los Angeles ranked as the tenth most populated city in the United States. In 1930, it was the fifth most populated city in the United States. The population more than doubled during that ten-year period.

The Roaring Twenties brought fame and fortune as Hollywood's star was rising. The first Hollywood premiere was in 1922. Harry Chandler put the blinking Hollywoodland sign above the Hollywood Hills in 1923. Everything was going L.A.'s way.

The Los Angeles Aqueduct (*Chinatown*) was built in 1913. Eleven years later, in 1924, city planners already knew they would soon need a bigger water supply.

On July 5, 1924, The Society of Civil Engineers recorded, "There was a lively discussion"[20] on how to solve the Colorado River problems. The river had many issues: flood control, conservation of flood waters and how to harness its power. I believe that everyone agreed on the necessity for the Hoover Dam. However, in the bigger picture of L.A. water, J.C. always saw Mexico as part of the solution while Mulholland focused further north on the Colorado River in Arizona.

Both J.C. Allison and William Mulholland learned engineering from books and experience. Mulholland became the Superintendent of Los Angeles Water and Power at age thirty-one. Mulholland laid out the water system for Los Angeles, and J.C. laid out the water system for the whole Imperial Valley. In addition, J.C. brought water into lower California. By the time

---

[20] *Electrical World*, Volume 84, "Civil Engineers Differ on Colorado Development," July 5, 1924, p 28.

J.C. was twenty-five years old, he became the Chief Engineer of the California Development Company, which eventual'y became the Imperial Irrigation District for lower California.

Later, the *San Diego Herald* said: "He is believed to be the youngest engineer ever to hold a position of this importance."[21]

The Imperial Irrigation District was 500,000 acres of farmland in the desert. Today, it produces 2.5 billion dollars in produce annually. Water was like gold.

Civil Engineers Differ on Colorado Development

A lively discussion took place at the recent San Francisco convention of the American Society of Civil Engineers over a paper by Col. William Kelly, chief engineer of the Federal Power Commission, on "The Colorado River Problem." A. P. Davis, J. C. Allison, F. H. Fowler, Louis C. Hill, E. C. LaRue, Major H. S. Bennion and William Mulholland presented views from different angles on power and irrigation needs in the Colorado River basin, some opposing and some defending the Boulder Cañon dam. The Mojave reservoir was advocated as a means of solving several of the more troublesome problems and was also vigorously decried as the revival of a scheme undesirable and ill-advised which was long ago abandoned as impracticable. Speakers mentioned the great importance of an agreement with Mexico before any extensive storage work was undertaken.

1924 "A lively discussion... J.C. Allison and William Mulholland"

[21] "J.C. Allison Civic Leader is Dead," Obituary, *San Diego Herald*, May 29, 1936

When the time came to provide more water for the city, J.C. had a plan to build an International Aqueduct using the Laguna Saluda as a reservoir which was across the border in Mexico. This would give access to both the Colorado River and the Gila River, doubling the water supply for half the expense. He called the plan the Allison-Forward Colorado River Plan.

While the plan had great potential, it also meant he had to include Mexico's agreement to a treaty as part of the plan. As in my pitch to CareMark Rx, when the question came up about Lloyd's of London, I was able to say, "They've already signed off." J.C. needed the same preparation for his pitch to the Metropolitan Water District and the State of California.

He was in Mexico City negotiating with the Mexican government when he wrote this letter to his daughter Estelle (Sissy), my dad's half-sister.

May 30, 1931

Dear Estelle:

Your nice letter came yesterday; it was a joy for me to receive it as I get awfully lonesome without my nice family around me... The first time I come here next, when you are not in school, I hope to bring you here just so you can meet these people and see other conditions under which people live... Am much encouraged that the great enterprise I am here on will turn out successfully. The President here has my maps etc, and I am to see him before I leave. The government hearings commence next week...[22]

These are very hard times little Sisy, and greater responsibilities are falling on all of us, yourself included...

---

[22] From family correspondence in the author's personal archives.

Give my love to all at home,
Your loving
Dady

He was under tremendous pressure to get this deal vetted and approved, yet he had time for family. The heat was still on when he wrote this letter to his mother-in-law six months later.

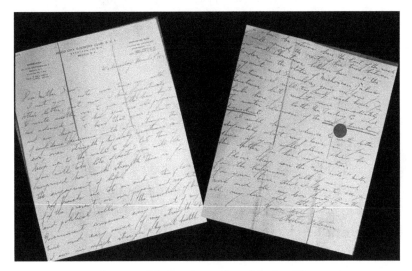

Letter to Mother Snow from Mexico City

December 9, 1931
Dear Mother Snow,
...Lotta has kept me advised as to how you are all progressing, and am happy to hear that your spirit of confidence remains with you stronger than ever; ones strength physically sometimes can't keep up to the will to go, but then if you will take lots of rest, you will be surprised how much strength there is for enjoyment of life....[23]

---

[23] From family correspondence in the author's personal archives.

What a beautiful example of creating heartfelt connections that stood him in good stead all his life.

That same year, J.C. wrote in *A History of Imperial Valley*:
I was fortunate in a continued advancement of position until the year 1912, when I became Chief Engineer and Assistant General Manager of all of the water affairs under the Receivership. In this capacity it fell to my lot to operate and maintain the entire water and flood protective system on both sides of the line [border] and to defend the Mexican properties.... During a part of this period, the Mexican Revolution was in effect... were both hazardous... and became at times dangerous on account of the revolutionary activities in the territory.
My heart was in the work of giving the best service to the water users on both sides of the line...[24]

How many successful men would show such heartfelt commitment to giving good service to all? J.C. was genuinely himself. That was one of the reasons he was so successful. When people realize you are genuine, they feel they can trust you.

"When people realize you are genuine, they feel that they can trust you."

When J.C. died, 500 Mexican citizens attended his funeral. What a testament to his connection to everyone he came in contact with.

Treat others the way you want to be treated.

---

[24] J.C. Allison, "Ownership by the People Becomes Vital," *The History of the Imperial Valley*, (Otis B. Tout, 1931), p 111.

You don't need to be perfect. It's OK for people to see your flaws. How you handle those flaws is what makes the difference.

Back to J.C.'s plan, by July, 1931, he had acquired permits allowing top engineers from both Mexico and the U.S. to conduct a study and vet all aspects of his plan.[25]

His cost projections looked good. A *Los Angeles Times* article dated July 20, 1931 stated:

> The understanding exists here that if the plan [the Allison-Forward Plan] can be embodied in an international treaty, the city of Los Angeles will be willing to accept it in lieu of the present costly project entailing the construction of an all-American canal to irrigate Imperial and Coachella valleys at an estimated cost of close to $40,000,000....[26]

This would be $40 million ($704 million today) in savings if Los Angeles agreed to my grandfather's plan. Mulholland's plan, the Colorado River Aqueduct, would cost $220 million ($3.9 billion today). The Allison plan cost $203 million (3.6 billion today), the equivalent of $300 million less than Mulholland's plan. Add the $700 million in savings above and you have an estimated 1 billion less than Mulholland's plan, in today's value.

J.C. was still hard at work five months later. In the same letter to his mother-in-law dated December 9, 1931, he went on to say:

> ...Negotiations and political calls on the members of this Government consume every minute of my time and every ounce of my strength.

---

[25] Jack Starr-Hunt, "New Colorado Plan," *Los Angeles Times*, July 20, 1931, p 5.
[26] Ibid.

I will try and reach home before Christmas but must come immediately back here for both the Trading Co. and the water business of the next International Aqueduct.[27]

Please keep on the "up -side", mother, for the happiness of all of us and for your own. And I hope I see you soon and all my dear family. Give them all my love, and lots for you.

Yours truly,

Chester Allison[28]

The first International Aqueduct was none other than the Panama Canal.

On the same scale as the Panama Canal treaty, J.C. negotiated with Mexico to protect U.S. interests when building the aqueduct using the Laguna Salada reservoir to bring water into Southern California.

Four months later, the Metropolitan Water District rushed to judgment before all the facts were in. They decided in favor of the Parker Dam route. The Allison-Forward Plan did not get a hearing. I surmise it was because Mexico was not on board yet.

In public companies, the CEO and Board of Directors have to answer to the shareholders. If something like this had happened in the modern business world, heads would have rolled.

Unfortunately, J.C. wasn't in modern business. He was in a political arena where other influences all too often come into the equation. He had the attention of Mexican officials, and he had banked on drawing the attention of the officials in the California state government as well.

My grandfather had worked for more than a year, and he had risked much of his personal savings. He wasn't giving up.

[27] From family correspondence in the author's personal archives.

[28] From family correspondence in the author's personal archives.

Days later, in January 1932, the Metropolitan Water Districts had several lawsuits filed "to prevent determination of the legality of the water district's bond issue..."[29] The contenders were trying to buy more time. My grandfather's plan was surely among the plaintiffs. He still needed to get Mexico on board.

Never give up. Whenever you can, you buy time. Particularly in something of this magnitude.

"Never give up. Whenever you can, you buy time."

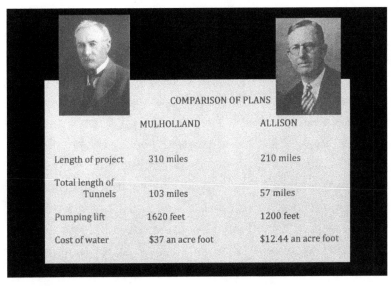

	MULHOLLAND	ALLISON
Length of project	310 miles	210 miles
Total length of Tunnels	103 miles	57 miles
Pumping lift	1620 feet	1200 feet
Cost of water	$37 an acre foot	$12.44 an acre foot

Comparison of Plans Parker Dam Route versus Allison-Forward Route

The battle went to the public with several full-page newspaper articles informing the public of the details about the Allison-Forward Plan and others, including routes, costs and estimated completion dates. Mulholland's Parker Dam route went too far north.[30]

---

[29] *Los Angeles Times*, Blocking the Aqueduct - January 28, 1932 p. A4.

[30] A. R. Sauer, "Allison-Forward Colorado River Plan To Put $50,000,000 At Work in County of San Diego," *San Diego Herald*, February 11,

According to a *Los Angeles Times* article dated February 11, 1932:

> The Allison-Forward project will give the cheapest water in the world to the Southern California coastal plain...the California coastal plain from Mexico to Santa Barbara will receive through the Allison-Forward project twice as much water as is possible by any other project having to do with the use of Colorado river water in this section of the Southwest.[31]

A few months later, in May 1932, after the engineers' study was complete, Mexican officials came around.

> "The party was greeted at Gov. Olachea's palace and there was a bountiful exchange of greetings between him and members of the party...the Mexican officials send greetings back to the people of California, expressed their interest in the Allison plan and said they hoped more such fine parties would come to visit their country, as it engendered a feeling of goodwill, as nothing else could."[32]

They were more than enthusiastic about the plan, since it would benefit Mexico as well as California. The *Los Angeles Times* recorded:

Now that Mexico was on board, J.C. and his compatriots directed all their energy toward influencing California to approve the plan. Funds in the amount of $220,000,000 had already been earmarked for the project. They only needed a nod to get started.

    1932, front page.

[31] Ibid.

[32] Chester G. Hanson, "Proposed Water Route," *Los Angeles Times*, May 29, 1932, p. 50.

AQUEDUCT PLAN APPROVED

Mexico Takes Tentative Action on International Colorado River Project

May 7th, 1932

MEXICO CITY, May 7. (Exclusive)—Announcement has been made here of the Mexican government's tentative approval of a plan submitted for the construction of an international aqueduct to start at a point on the Colorado River about ten miles south of the California-Lower California border line, and which will extend in a northwesterly direction a total distance of 210 miles, seventy of which are in Mexico, crossing into California at the Tia Juana-San Diego border gateway.

Negotiations with the government have been conducted for some time past by J. C. Allison, consulting engineer of San Diego, Cal., author of the international project as a substitute for the proposed aqueduct from Parker, Ariz., to the Los Angeles zone.

The international route would, in matter and it now is pending study on the part of other governmental departments.

The international route would originate at the Colorado, its flow being diverted ten miles south of the border at a point that would lead directly to Laguna Salada, where a reservoir would be constructed and the water _____

1932 AQUEDUCT PLAN APPROVED

Negotiations with the government have been conducted for some time by J. C. Allison, consulting engineer of San Diego, Cal. author of the International Project as a substitute for the proposed aqueduct from Parker, Ariz., to the Los Angeles zone.[33]

On May 29, 1932, the Los Angeles Times quoted my grandfather: "All we are doing," he said, "is to ask the State of California to investigate our plan thoroughly."[34]

Another article in the Los Angeles Times stated:

What proved to be a remarkable mass demonstration of the interest in the Allison-Forward

---

[33] "Aqueduct Plan Approved," Los Angeles Times, May 8, 1932, p. 1.

[34] Chester G. Hanson, "Proposed Water Route," Los Angeles Times, May 29, 1932, p. 50.

plan...an impressive climax here late this afternoon at a reception in the Palace of His Excellency, Agustin Olachea, Governor of Lower California....The demonstration began in San Diego at 8 o'clock this morning, when a great motor caravan of 143 automobiles, carrying 700 men and women from Southern California communities...water can be brought to the Coast from the Colorado River cheaper and more efficiently than by any other route known. Allison pointed out that his plan draws water from the Colorado at a closer point to the coast than any other plan advocated.[35]

Inspections of water route May 28, 1932. Both Los Angeles Times articles. In attendance, representative for Gov. Rolph and Lieut. Gov. Frank Merriam who became Governor of California in 1934.

Mulholland was thirty years my grandfather's senior, yet my grandfather had come up with a plan that would provide double the water for much less cost. He sweetened the deal.

Like my bid for the CareMark Rx account, J.C. put several principles into play:

---

[35] Ibid.

- Pay your dues—He had put in 10,000 hours in the river systems of the Western U.S. and Mexico. He worked hard to stay abreast of new discoveries and inventions.
- I Can—He had the chutzpa to go after a treaty with a foreign government.
- Where there is chaos, there is opportunity—Los Angeles needed water and emotions ran high. J.C. had proven his ability to calm the chaos when it came to supplying water.
- Luck is where preparation meets opportunity—He stayed in the know, watching for opportunities and maintaining relationships. He stayed in the game.
- People do business with people they like—Heartfelt, hard-working and dedicated, J.C. had labored alongside, dined with and hung out with many people involved in the process. Whether at The Jonathan Club or camping on the banks of a river in Mexico, he felt comfortable anywhere and with pretty much anyone. Just as important, they felt comfortable with him.

Luck is where preparation meets opportunity.

The Mexican government backed the Allison Forward Plan. California taxpayers saw the massive benefits of the Allison-Forward Plan. Engineers vetted the plan. What was left?

The ruling of the Supreme Court. The game's not over until it's over.

Mentoring Tori

Tori has always been an inclusive child who made sure that everyone is taken care of. Many times, I've seen her draw children on the periphery into activities. She naturally gravitates toward them to make them feel a part of everyone.

Being a team player is authentically who she is with her skill, drive and coachability. At times her coach has to call her off a ball because she is full speed ahead and about to collide with something. She is a libero, which means she is all defense in the back row where she digs and passes to the setter. She's also a freshman on a team of all sophomores.

Tori

Like her brother and sister, Tori does not have a "B" game, only an "A" game when it comes to sports. With our heritage, it is no surprise! Each year Tori's club team goes to Las Vegas to compete. This was her first year playing all defense as the libero. She went after everything! For the first time in several years, her team went 7-0 against some good opponents. At the end of each day, Tori would walk out, all smiles, with her knees wrapped in ice like she had been in a battle.

To watch Tori's Varsity highlights from her freshman year, go to YouTube: Tori Allison Hagan, Varsity Highlights, Freshman year

Tori Allison Hagan - Varsity Highlights - Freshman year
https://www.youtube.com/watch?v=qv0XA46v5fA

A LUCY MOMENT
Hurricanes and Alligators

My destination was Kiawah Island, South Carolina, where me and "the boys," my partners Bob Dubraski and Frank McKenna, were going to spend a few days at an elite golf resort.

My plane took off from LAX, connecting through Atlanta to an airport near Kiawah Island. Near the end of the flight, we encountered turbulent weather. We came close to landing in Atlanta when the plane tipped sideways, causing the pilot to abort the landing. We circled for a while and then they announced that we were being diverted to a regional airport in Florida.

When we landed, a cheerful voice over the intercom announced that all flights were grounded. I looked at a map and saw I was a 3.5-hour drive from Kiawah Island. Rather than wait until tomorrow, I decided to rent a car and be there for dinner. I have pioneer blood in my veins. What could happen?

On the highway, it was raining so hard I could barely see. Crossing that lonely stretch in southern Georgia, I had an idea that getting off the highway wasn't a good idea. This California girl could end up in *Deliverance* territory (cue the banjos).

After a long grueling drive, I arrived at the resort and checked into my room. I freshened up and went to find the guys in the bar.

When I arrived, they grinned at me, and McKenna said, "You made it."

I could tell they were worried as they were sipping cocktails!

We woke up to clear skies the next day. I don't golf, but the outfits were cute and I had a nice set of clubs, so I looked the part. The guys tolerated me because I had entertainment value.

I would get out of the cart and whack at the ball a few times, then stand aside for the next person. Then the ball landed near an 8-foot bunker. I kept whacking at the ball and it kept coming back, the golf version of racket ball. Finally, Frank rescued me by saying, "Time to call it a day," in between laughs!

Another time, I hit the ball too soon, and it went directly toward the foursome ahead of us. Terrified someone would be hurt, I yelled "Head!" instead of *for*... or is it *four* or *fore*? Anyway, you can imagine the guys' reactions.

In my defense, I was thinking about my ball hitting someone in the forehead. The fore just dropped off. The guys in the foursome kept looking over and smiling when our group arrived at the clubhouse for a drink.

I didn't know it until that day, but Kiawah is known for its "healthy population of American Alligators," the local euphemism for gigantic. Around the tenth hole, a granddaddy lay nearby, enjoying the sun, while we teed off.

When I caught sight of it, my heart went into my throat. I turned to Bob Dubraski and asked, "Doesn't that thing make you nervous?"

Grinning, he shook his head, then set his ball. Glancing at me before he lined up, he replied, "All I have to do is out run you."

I laughed, then thought, *Wait a minute...*

The moral of the story: if you're golfing near the southern coast, always be prepared to outrun your Partne's. And if you're in the middle of a bunch of guys, don't yell, "Head!"

CHAPTER 6

Know Your Niche

Focus on identifying your target audience, communicating an authentic message and project yourself as an "expert" within your niche.[36] *~Kim Garst*

A specialist always seems more valuable than a generalist. Take doctors, for example. A heart specialist's pay scale is much higher than general practitioner or primary care provider. And

---

[36] https://quotefancy.com/quote/1580320/Kim-Garst-Focus-on-identifying-your-target-audience-communicating-an-authentic-message

wouldn't you rather take your ailing car to a transmission specialist or muffler specialist than a local garage that doesn't seem to specialize in anything?

Because I specialized in medical groups early on, I developed expertise and relationships that launched my career to high levels very quickly.

Luck is where preparation meets opportunity.

———————————————

During my first insurance brokerage job with Frank Weston, I saw firsthand the benefits of working a niche. Frank specialized in School Districts, and he kept clients for years, decades even. When I landed Friendly Hills Medical Group, I knew right away that I would specialize in medical groups.

"A niche is a specialized segment of the market for a particular kind of product or service."

Anyone in sales should be on the lookout for an opportunity to place themselves in a niche market. A niche is a specialized segment of the market for a particular kind of product or service. As much as you can, place yourself so you are in demand for your knowledge.

I set myself apart from my competition by putting together a survey of benefits for the medical groups. I used this survey as a door opener to sit down with the respective CEOs and share my company's benefits information. I would place their company name in the survey and gave them the results.

Once they saw the great value I provided, I started to earn their trust. When the time came to renew their employee benefits, I would place a bid. Because they had seen me provide valuable service beforehand, I had an advantage over other bidders, and I usually won their business.

"Once they saw the great value I provided, I started to earn their trust."

Another way of setting yourself apart is by having the latest news and information. The Medical Groups all wanted to know what the other groups were doing. In this kind of specialty, a company will hire you because they don't want to be left out of the up and coming trends that their friendly competitors are implementing. Make yourself indispensable.

While I was a Partner at McKenna & Associates, the large brokers were not in our niche. Soon after I retired, Mercer had the opportunity to come into the medical group market and take a couple of my largest clients from AON because no one else specialized in employee benefits for medical groups.

Fron left: Lotta, Mother Snow, J.C. Mexico City

Niche markets are small arenas where the players come to know each other. Sometimes, people shift from company to company, creating a unique situation where the same people will cross back and forth from partnerships to competitors, and back again. When working in niche markets, specialized principles apply.

First, observe the behaviors and relationships of others in your same niche. Know the players and how they fit together. In my niche, people often switched companies, so someone competing for a contract one year might be on my team the next year. Getting to know these people means understanding an individual's strengths and weaknesses. When putting together a proposal, understanding what makes key players tick is a vital skill for creating a win, whether that individual is working with you or competing against you.

"Observe the behaviors and relationships of others in your same niche."

Second, never put down a competitor. I've seen people gossip and spread the latest rumors in a derogatory way. This always ends up with the tale bearer looking bad to the client. Take the high road and stay on the positive side of the conversation. When people hear someone putting a colleague down, they immediately wonder what that person might be saying about them as well. This is a no-win move.

"Never put down a competitor."

People do business with people they like.

Third, never burn a bridge. The very person you have offended could end up being your next boss. This is a general rule of thumb in business, but especially in a niche business. The managed care healthcare industry was a small world. During the years when risk was shifting from the HMO's to providers, employees constantly switched between the two sides. You might go head to head with someone to win a contract one month and end up in a cubicle next to them three months later.

"Never burn a bridge."

No matter how much you dislike your current situation, always leave on good terms. All too often, I have seen people leave a job with a scorched-earth approach, only to have their actions come back to haunt them years later.

Fourth, stay up to date on the latest niche news. Be the person everyone looks forward to seeing because they know you will have updates. I landed more than one contract because the previous service provider was asleep at the wheel and failed to inform their client of the latest changes.

"Stay up to date on the latest niche news."

1987 HERITAGE

"Entering the game had
given him the chance to show
his value to the world."

When Politics Are Involved, You Can't Win

J.C. Allison also had a niche market. He had spent 10,000 hours on the Colorado River. He knew its soil and the engineering aspects of water flow like few others. He showed value to people in the industry, and he stayed up with the latest developments. He knew how to put together a plan, vet that plan, and then sweeten the deal.

"He knew how to put together a plan, vet that plan, and then sweeten the deal."

After Mexico approved the Allison-Forward plan in May, 1932, a caravan of 700 cars went to the Mexican governor's palace to show support. J.C. was rolling high. It looked like the tide had finally turned in his favor. He headed for Washington, D.C. to get the international treaty approved.

A week later, the Supreme Court of California upheld the bond approving Mulholland's plan. Once that news came out, my grandfather's story went dark.

What a loss, you might say. More than a year of hard work and $30,000 of his own money down the drain—in the middle of the Great Depression, no less.

I don't want to minimize my grandfather's disappointment during this time. He was understandably devastated. On the other hand, the name of Joseph Chester Allison had been all over the newspapers from Los Angeles to San Diego and across the border into Mexico. His plan had brilliance and expertise unmatched by anyone else in the race. Entering the game had given him the chance to show his value to the world.

**"Entering the game had given him the chance
to show his value to the world."**

At that point, J.C. became the go-to expert in matters of the Colorado River and water supply. He continued his consulting business with offices in San Diego and Los Angeles where he consulted for multiple water companies.

He also had several other innovations in his wheelhouse. By 1930, he had figured out how to maximize the water output from a drilled well. A 1930 *Los Angeles Times* article stated,

> One of the water achievements of Chester Allison, the engineer who has proposed a new route for the Boulder Dam water, is a new way of drilling wells in the desert. He makes wells yield several times the normal amount of water by forcing tons of sand and cement down the pipe hole, creating an area of loose filter.[37]

In today's world, we call that marketable expertise. J.C. had it in spades.

Luck is where preparation meets opportunity.

His connection with the water supply gave him the opportunity to lease 100,000 acres for planting cotton in Baja California. That led to his building warehouses. In 1928, he had a tideland lease from the Port of San Diego and built a 30,000 square foot warehouse (with four more to follow). He leased them to those exporting and importing out of the Port of San Diego. That led to his building a railroad for goods transportation from Mexicali to the Gulf of Mexico. He followed in his

[37] Harry Carr, "Desert Wells," The Lancer, *Los Angeles Times*, September 3, 1930, A1

grandfather's footsteps, as Robert Allison was involved with building a railroad in the late 1800s.

Everything started from his niche.

From a business standpoint, the plans of my grandfather and William Mulholland become a fascinating study. In business, you always want to master the knowns—the verifiable information that help a potential buyer overcome objections.

"The knowns are the verifiable information that help a potential buyer overcome objections."

Remember, you control the uncontrollable by going through every possible known objection. The unknowns are out of your control.

If I were sitting across the table from J.C. during his presentation, here is what I would want to know.

The Knowns

1. Are the head engineers qualified?

Both engineers were experienced and well respected in their field. Every newspaper article or write-up in Society of Civil Engineers or other publications spoke highly of my grandfather's engineering experience and ability to solve complex problems involving water resources. While both engineers were qualified, in 1928, just three years before the L.A. water race, Mulholland's St. Francis Dam catastrophically failed, resulting in 431 deaths.

2. What is the proposed cost differential between the two plans?

Mulholland's plan would cost $220 million[38]. My grandfather's plan would have cost $203 million.[39] The difference in

---

[38] *San Diego Herald*, February 1932.

[39] Ibid.

today's dollars: $300 million. My grandfather's plan also eliminated the need for an All-American Canal with another estimated $40 million[40] in savings, $704 million in today's dollars. No one disputed that my grandfather's plan would be better for the taxpayers.

3. Had a proposed international treaty like this been successful in the past?

In 1931, the Panama Canal Treaty had been in place for fifteen years without any problems. This treaty provided major benefits to U.S. shipping, saving both time and expense.

4. Had an independent study verified the claims and safety of the plan?

On July 20, 1931, The *L.A. Times* reported:

Because of its international aspect, the Mexican Foreign Office, working jointly with the International Water Commission, has used its influence to extend the necessary permit authorizing engineers to make a detailed and minute study of the proposed development which, if found to embody the advantages claimed for it, may form part of the contemplated international water treaty.[41]

Mexico and the International Water Commission requested a second opinion to determine if my grandfather's claims were true.

---

[40] Ibid.

[41] Jack Starr-Hunt, "New Colorado Plan Advanced," *Los Angeles Times*, July 1931.

5. How would this affect Mexico?

> An international water treaty between the two
> nations, will do much to eliminate the vexing issue
> that has existed between the two countries [United
> States and Mexico] for a number of years over the
> distribution of the water supply of the Colorado
> without infringing on the benefits to be derived by
> the construction of the Boulder Dam.[42]

The Allison-Forward Plan would aid international rela-
tions by eliminating future dispute' over water rights between
the United States and Mexico.

6. What would be collateral benefits if the proposed
    plan was selected?

> "Besides savings in proposed canals, [my grandfather's
> plan] will also solve the problem of flood control on the lower
> river, it is contended, saving many millions which otherwise must
> be spent by the two governments".[43]

In 1932, $2 million would be savings of $35 million in
today's dollars. The *L.A. Times* said, "...the Allison scheme as
presented to the Mexican government provides for the possibility of a complete conservation of all available waters of the
Colorado River."[44]

It would capture water from the Gila River, which is 500
miles long, and store those millions of gallons in the Laguna
Salada. This plan would also solve flood problems and prevent
water from being wasted.

---

[42] Ibid.

[43] *Protection and Development of Lower Colorado Basin*, August 15, 1924, Part
    5, p 825.

[44] "New Colorado Plan Advanced," *Los Angeles Times*, July 1931.

7. What was the outcome of the independent study?

On May 8, 1932, the *Los Angeles Times* released this article entitled "Aqueduct Plan Approved":

> The international route would, in the opinion of those sponsoring it, cost very much less than the estimated amount of $220,000,000 already bonded for the all-American channel, and would benefit much more of Southern California without detracting from the benefit Los Angeles would derive from the Parker route channel.
>
> The plan has been endorsed and approved by a majority of high officials." If a majority of high officials in the Mexican government had approved it ten months after the permits were pulled, then it is my opinion that the proposal had been successfully vetted (the stated savings/claims etc. were validated by a joint, international commission of engineers).[45]

8. What were the overall confirmed benefits of the proposed plan?

My grandfather's plan would provide twice the water of Mulholland's aqueduct at half the cost of any other proposals. Clearly the Allison-Forward Colorado River Plan was the most cost-effective and efficient option.

The Unknowns

    a. Whether his plan would get approval from all concerned

My grandfather had three major hurdles to clear: Mexico's approval, Washington D.C.'s approval of the International Treaty, and the approval of the Metropolitan Water District. As

---

[45] "Aqueduct Plan Approved," *Los Angeles Times*, May 8, 1932, p 1.

soon as my grandfather got approval from Mexico, he left Mexico City and went straight to Washington D.C. However, the Supreme Court of California ruled before he could complete his mission. They upheld the bond issue, allowing the Metropolitan Water District to proceed with their choice, the Parker Dam Route.

b. Whether he would get a fair shake

Being a business owner who has worked with some of the largest companies in my area of business, the lack of logic in the outcome indicates that unknown factors influenced the Metropolitan Water District's decision. J.C. couldn't analyze or predict whether he would get a fair shake when it came to political machinations.

In the end, it didn't matter if my grandfather promised them the moon and the stars. They were going to do what they wanted to do.

When there are politics involved, you can't win.
~Anonymous

MENTORING MICHAEL

I have always encouraged Michael to work with mergers and acquisitions in some shape or form. Mergers and acquisitions provide niche skills with a wide potential for learning since they also have complications and challenges that need solutions.

The last half of my career, I also worked with companies that were paid handsomely by Wall Street to acquire other companies. The cycle for acquisitions varies by industry, so study the past in a particular industry to establish a pattern you can plan around. The insurance brokerage industry has an eight-year cycle for acquisitions.

Mergers and acquisitions will not only separate you from your competition but also give you valuable connections with the higher ups. Those relationships can be key to progress in your career because as the cycle continues, someone you know could become a potential recruiter for a position that supports your career goals.

A LUCY MOMENT
AK-47's in Los Angeles

Everyone remembers where they were on April 29, 1992, the day the L.A. riots started. They began exactly sixty years after J.C.'s race to bring water to Los Angeles, from April 29 to May 4. I inadvertently ended up in the middle of it.

The drama started when four white LAPD officers were accused of using excessive force in the arrest of Rodney King. A videotape showed the officers beating Rodney King while he lay on the ground.

As soon as the not-guilty verdict came out, mayhem broke loose in South Central Los Angeles, including rioting, looting, assault, arson and murder. The estimate of property damage was $1 billion. Then-Governor Pete Wilson called in two thousand of the California Army National Guard to restore order. Sixty-three people died. Two thousand were injured.

During this six-day period, I had a meeting set with Steve Barker, Vice President of Human Resources at Centinela Hospital. Steve was a client who had become a friend. I first met him when he worked at Brea Community Hospital where I sold him an employee benefits package. As long as I made him look good, whenever he switched hospitals, he took me with him.

That day, I was on my way to a routine renewal meeting. Steve, his assistant Debbie and I typically went out to lunch afterward and had a lot of laughs. Their sense of humor was just like mine. The stories would go on non-stop for more than an hour. Of course, I always had some new ones tucked away—all true, by the way. Humor was always the key.

Only today I didn't feel like laughing. People in L.A. were locked inside their homes, scared for their lives while pandemonium reigned in the streets. I had a knot in my stomach, but I figured that Sepulveda Boulevard in Inglewood was a safe distance from the rioting. Besides, if Steve Barker could go to work and not be afraid, then I wasn't going to be afraid!

Everything went as planned until my gas gauge went past E as I reached Sepulveda. A few minutes later, my car engine skipped. I had two choices: pull to the side of Sepulveda and be a sitting duck, or go down a side street. I chose the side street.

My car died before I'd gone a block.

I called Steve. "I'm running late because I ran out of gas. I'm so close I can almost see the hospital from here."

He gasped. "You're kidding me, right?"

"I can see the sign for a gas station. I'll be there soon."

I heard him say, "Be careful!" as I took the phone from my ear to disconnect.

Looking around, I saw no one on the street and got out of the car to walk. My $600 shoes crunched on broken glass bottles. The store across the street had smashed windows. Suddenly, I realized I was in the belly of the beast.

What could I do? Only one thing: keep on walking.

I was alone in a war zone with my blonde hair, black suit and high heels, stumbling in a hurry to ask for some gas. Outside the gas station stood two burly, black-bearded men with a Middle Eastern look about them. They were both holding AK-47's. (I kid you not!)

Panic tinged my voice when I called out to the closest one, "Hi, I ran out of gas. Can you please help me?"

The two guys looked at each other. Then they both looked me up and down. After another meeting of the minds without words, one of them headed inside. The one closest to me nodded and said in a thick accent, "He'll be back."

I wasn't sure if that was a good thing or not.

The second guy returned holding a red gas can, and I pulled out a twenty. Seven minutes later, I not only had gas in my car but two armed escorts had put it in for me.

They actually smiled a little when the engine roared to life. With a wave and a wobbly "Thank you!" I turned around and broke the speed limit getting out of there.

When I finally reached Steve's office, my hands were still shaking. Steve was behind his desk and Debbie in a chair across from him.

Debbie got up to hug me. "Are you all right?" she asked.

I drew in a breath and nodded. "Two guys with AK-47's were at the gas station. They escorted me back to my car."

Steve let out a gasp and shook his head with his famous eye roll. "Only you!"

Debbie got me some hot coffee, and we settled down to work. The connection between the three of us grew some roots that day. We'd always been about the business and the laughs, but after that there was something more.

My co-worker, Joanne, always told me, "If there's ever any trouble, I want to be with you. You have a guardian angel."

Knowing what I know now, I believe she's right.

CHAPTER 7

Build Trust

All things being equal, people will do business with, and refer business to, those people they know, like and trust.[46] ~Bob Burg,

On a chilly January morning, I sat at my desk going through some reports. Part of my mind was on a lunch meeting I had that day. I slid my fingernail down the page. *Wait a minute.* I went back a few pages to cross check the numbers… and forgot to breathe.

---

[46] https://www.goodreads.com/work/quotes/1873970-the-go-giver-a-little-story-about-a-powerful-business-idea

I had made a miscalculation when I translated a rate on a recent proposal. Worse, the proposal had gone for Board approval two days before. I sat there, sick to my stomach. Based on that figure, I had recommended that Friendly Hills move away from a carrier they had been with for fifteen years.

I was twenty-eight, and I could see my career flashing before my eyes. What was I going to do? Closing my eyes, I forced myself to breathe slowly and deeply. While I was still in high school, my dad taught me to do the right thing, not because it will get you somewhere, but because it is the right thing.

"Do the right thing, not because it will get you somewhere, but because it is the right thing."

Me salmon fishing on the Rogue River with UM6A

Thirty seconds later, I made an appointment with Friendly Hills' CEO, Dr. Barnett (Ugh!). Rescheduling my lunch date, I headed for his rather intimidating office and told him what had happened. I then suggested a solution: stay with the current carrier with a rate reduction (not nearly as great as originally proposed).

Dr. Barnett sat still for a moment (while my stomach churned). Finally, he said, "Everyone makes mistakes, Therese. Because of the way you handled it, you will keep our business."

PHEW!

Not only did I keep his business, but years later, Dr. Barnett appointed me to the Board of Directors of his non-profit.

Own up to your mistakes. Come up with a solution

Needless to say, when I fell on my sword with the carrier I had misrepresented, he "ripped me a new one." Well, that goes with the territory. At least he couldn't fire me.

Dr. Barnett was one of the leading CEO's of the California Medical Groups. If I had chosen to hide my mistake, from that day forward my career with the Medical Groups would have been severely limited. During that transition period, the groups were sharing best practices and discussed what was working and wasn't working for them. I did not want to be added to the Not Working list! When you specialize in a niche, the world is very small.

"When you specialize in a niche, the world is very small."

Your reputation is the main thing in any profession as well as in your personal life. Always take the high road, especially anyone who is a lawyer or an insurance broker. Those careers already have a negative stereotype to overcome. A person with integrity will rise.

Here is my personal list of business ethics that took me to the top:

- When you don't know the answer to a question, say so. Don't bullshit.
- It's ok not to have an answer. Just make sure you find the answer and get back to them.

If you don't know the answer, say so.

———————————

- Triple check any numbers in a presentation.

If you get into a meeting with a glaringly wrong number, you take two steps back in credibility.

- When you make a mistake, own up to it, fall on your sword with all involved, then present a solution.

Presenting a solution will save the day. Give the person you're talking to a sigh of relief when they realize you've got them covered. Let people know they can depend on you to come to them promptly with a problem, even before they find it themselves.

- Put yourself in their shoes.

If you are proposing something to a decision maker, put yourself on their side of the table and think of questions their higher-ups will ask. Give them answers, so they feel prepared. In doing so, you will stave off a lot of objections and show you are on top of your game. You are, ultimately, part of the deal, so establishing credibility is important.

- Always dance with the partner who brought you to the dance.

This shows loyalty and integrity. Had I continued in the business, I would have stayed loyal to McKenna because he believed in me and provided the platform for me, a woman, to be successful.

Always dance with the partner who brought you to the dance.

———————————

Today, young people change jobs too frequently. Michael has been with his employer for seven years now. My advice to him has been that this will make him stand out in the company and help him climb the ladder.

If you are shooting for the job of your dreams, show loyalty to your current employer. Build tenure. Trust me, when that position you've dreamed of comes around, and you have paid your dues, you will be hired. Tenure is like putting deposits into a bank of trust.

When you decide to change companies, trust you've built with your current employer will become currency with your next employer. They want to know they can trust you to stay with the company after they invest in training you. Be the exception, not the rule. It will pay off in the long run.

"Be the exception, not the rule. It will pay off in the long run."

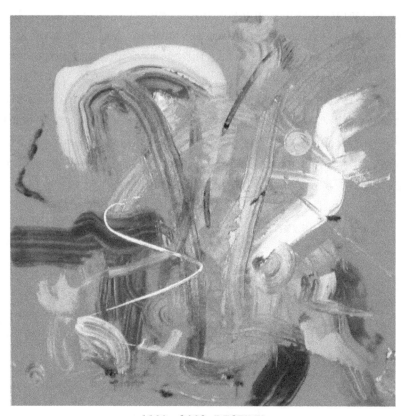

1999 - 2003 DESTINY

"It is easy to forget who you
are doing it for."

The Mystery of the Robbery

After May, 1932, the press went dark about my grandfather's Allison-Forward Plan. He also left very little technical documentation besides the few details that were in the *San Diego Herald* article. His original route map, family correspondence from Mexico City and, of course, his picture with the President of Mexico were at his home in La Jolla.

However, no correspondence on negotiation discussions with Mexico, Washington D.C., or, quite frankly, anyone else were among his papers. Most importantly, the actual detailed proposal of his plan was nowhere to be found. They didn't have computers or the Internet back then, so paper was everything.

Treating this research like I would when I was in business, I was able to put together the pieces from this century- old story because I had access to the *Los Angeles Times* and, of course, it probably helps that I think like my grandfather!

My grandfather's plan cost considerably less. He had a proven track record, and he had Mexico on board. I wonder what kept him from winning the deal. That's the billion-dollar question.

On January 30, 1932, a *Los Angeles Times* article stated: Motorship Molokai to enter West American Trade…initial sailing from Harbor set for February 5 [1932]… there will be a monthly service to Los Angeles, San Diego, San Juan Del Cabo, Mazatlan, Acapulco…

The Molokai is being operated under charter to the Marine Trading Corporation of San Diego, J.C. Allison, president.[47]

This is the shipping that J.C. referenced in his letter to Mother Snow dated December 9, 1931, two months earlier. His negotiations with Mexico for Foreign Trade were successful.

People do business with people they like.

Many times over the course of my career, I have encountered politics outside of my control. Once, I lost a huge life insurance plan with one of my largest clients because the decision maker's brother-in-law worked for a rival carrier. Nothing would change that situation. When politics are involved, you can't win. The only recourse is to move on.

That's what J.C. did. He simply went to the next things in his path: his consulting business, agriculture, shipping and warehousing. He attracted business partners and investors because he had built trust with his community. He was the Golden Boy, and whatever he touched turned to gold.

His kryptonite: he was a workaholic. He literally worked himself to a premature death. Four years later, in 1936, he died of a heart attack after swimming in the La Jolla Cove.

After he died, the safe was robbed in his office at the Allison Warehouse in the Port of San Diego, and all its contents taken. According to my dad, the family knew the safe contained official letters and documents from the Allison-Forward Plan.

Who took them? That mystery will never be solved.

---

[47] "New Freighter Service Booked - Motorship Molokai to enter West Mexican Trade," *Los Angeles Times,* January 30, 1932, p 11.

My dad lost his father at the age of six. The Allison family was brokenhearted.

The Allison family has a history of heart disease, and stress is a risk factor for heart attacks. After more than a year of grueling work putting together his Allison-Forward Plan, J.C. immediately immersed himself in many enterprises including building a railroad and founding a bank in Calexico.

Like J.C., I worked long hours in a high-stress career, so I can relate to his drive and hyper-focus. My career gave me a lot of satisfaction. However, without balance this level of stress can have a negative impact on your health and that has a negative impact on your family. At the end of the day, it is easy to forget who you are doing it for.

"It is easy to forget who you are doing it for."

On June 1, 1936, the *Los Angeles Times* published this article honoring my grandfather, J.C. Allison:

> California owes much of its present position in the galaxy of States to the efforts of its civil engineers and irrigation experts who have taken a major part in developing its natural resources and turning its once desert wastes into fertile farms and productive orchards.
>
> Nowhere has their work been more marked than in the reclamation of the Colorado Desert and the establishing there in the great Imperial Valley of the most comprehensive food supplying area in the United States.
>
> And among the names of those who will always be associated with this epochal development, that of J.C. Allison, consulting engineer, organizer of irrigation districts and promoter of foreign trade, will occupy a conspicuous space.

Mr. Allison's death has deprived Southern
California of another of its inspiring constructive
workers…and his memory (will be) honored by
all who have faith in the future of California.[48]

The *Calexico Chronicle* stated: "He had the vision of a pioneer… He faced tremendous obstacles – and sometimes lost - but his optimism never faded."[49]

Like Mulholland Drive, this story twists and turns. It was a risky proposition, far riskier than my grandfather realized.

---

[48] "J.C. Allison," *Los Angeles Times*, June 1936, A4 p 1.
[49] R.H., *Calexico Chronicle*. The italicized quote was from 1916, and the full article was written circa 1944. No other information available.

Mentoring Jamie

I learned many life lessons from playing team sports, and that made me a firm believer that team sports prepare our young people for life. For me, I learned to Play for Keeps and pull out all of the stops playing team sports. I see the same in my kids. They Play for Keeps and always leave everything on the ice or court.

Michael started playing hockey when he was five. As a result, Jamie was always at the ice rink. When she was four, we put her on skates. She was fearless as she fell. She never wanted to give up.

She started competing in singles events about a year later, at age five. One competition early on, she looked the part wearing an ice-blue skating dress with crystals on the front. Her blonde hair was braided and pinned up, and the finishing touch: her big blue eyes.

Nothing is more nerve racking than waiting in the stands while your little girl is about to perform. She stepped onto the ice and started out strong. About halfway through the program, she caught her toe pick and fell forward, onto her face.

We all gasped. My stomach sank. I waited for her to start crying. She got up and continued her program. When the crowd cheered for her, she waved with both hands and smiled as if it was all a part of her program. That was when I knew she had found her sport.

When Tori was old enough to participate in a sport, she wanted to be like her big sister, so I put her in a pair of ice skates. After about a year and a half, she said that it hurt when she fell. That moment I knew that figure skating was not her sport. All kids are different, and I just wanted mine to find their passion.

In the sport of singles figure skating, only a handful of elite skaters make it to the U.S. Championships. A skater who wants to make it to Nationals has to switch to synchronized skating.

Jamie

Jamie started synchronized skating when she was eight. In synchronized skating sixteen skaters perform figure skating in unison. Because of my background in team sports, I was happy to see Jamie on a team. Team sports were key in my ultimate success in business. I not only learned leadership and how to work as a team, but how to win and lose as a team. As a girl, I also learned confidence, commitment, communication and how to trust.

Trust is key in synchronized skating. They are truly interconnected. Each skater builds trust with those around because each one is dependent on the other.

As Jamie progressed, she started skating at the senior level. When she was fourteen, a coach tapped her on the shoulder in a free skating session and asked her to try out for a team called California Gold. She was the youngest on the team, but she was a strong skater and consistently asked her coach, "What do I have to do in order to be put in?"

A total of twenty were on the team and only sixteen on the ice.

Middle: Jamie and I at her 2014 National's; Left and Right: Jamie at the 2016 World Championships in Budapest

Eventually, her coach put her in. This was her first time competing in the long program. Trust between teammates was essential as their routine included lifts. Three skaters lift one skater above their heads and rotate 360 degrees, while moving forward. They then had to bring that skater back down without getting sliced by a blade. That maneuver is both amazing and terrifying to watch. Parents watching had a collective sigh of relief once the team completed their lifts.

During college, Jamie skated for Miami University in Ohio. In 2016, Jamie and her team skated for the USA at the 2016 World Championships in Budapest, Hungary. They placed 8th out of 26 teams. Mexico was also in the competition and placed 18th.

To view these moments, Go to YouTube:
WSSC 2016 Budapest - USA 2 (Miami University) - Free Skating
https://www.youtube.com/watch?v=1e--UhK_WxQ&t=87s

WSSC 2016 Budapest - Mexico (Merging Edge) - Free Skating
https://www.youtube.com/watch?v=2hHwmi28mKY&t=177s

A LUCY MOMENT
Chez Cary

Recently, I had lunch with Jim Hillman and Diane Bailey. I met them through the Unified Medical Group Association (UMGA). Over coffee, Jim reminded me of the time I tried to impress him and his wife, Judy, with a 5-star dinner. Judy worked for PacifiCare Health Systems, one of the top HMO's in California at the time.

I wanted to work with Jim's member medical groups, and I also wanted to land PacifiCare as a client. I rarely got a chance to pitch two major companies at the same time. This meeting was a pretty big deal.

That night, I wore a blue silk dress with a tie at the waist and pearls, of course. I was wearing my selling suit and, believe me, I checked my shoes.

Wear your selling suit, and check your shoes.

I had reservations at a high-end restaurant called Chez Cary in Orange. Back in the day, it was one of the only 5-star restaurants around with a reputation for the best chef in town—and a price tag to match. I was pulling out all the stops!

On the way to the restaurant, it started raining. I wasn't concerned. It was going to be a good night.

While my husband and I were driving, a restaurant critic came on the radio, reviewing Orange County restaurants. I wasn't paying much attention until he said "Chez Cary," then he informed us that the restaurant had changed owners and the food was not good, at all.

My heart sank. I've worked through a lot of curveballs before, but this one was a whopper.

When we arrived at the restaurant at 6:30, the parking lot had only two cars, and one of those belonged to Jim and Judy. A valet took our car. For a moment, I wondered if, maybe, all of the cars were valeted in the back.

Inside, we quickly spotted Jim and Judy...and one other couple...the only people in the entire dining room.

At this point, I figured, *I'm not going to be able to tap dance my way out of this one.*

We ordered drinks. At least the service was 5-star. The wait staff didn't have anyone else to pay attention to. As soon as we had a drink, I fessed up and told them what we had heard on the drive. Jim and Judy started laughing. From that point on, every food snafu was funny. The other couple in the dining room started giving us curious looks. So did the waiter. We only laughed more.

Sometimes all you can do is be authentic and use humor. Sometimes, you've just got to laugh. (Oh, and I did land Judy's business after all!)

CHAPTER 8

The Velvet Glove

*Being both soft and strong is a combination very few
have mastered.*[50] ~Anonymous

Like Reese Witherspoon, Sandra Bullock and Lucille Ball,
I learned early in my career to use a Velvet Glove. Make people
laugh (Velvet), but also be smart (Glove). I once heard that
Lucille Ball was dumb as a fox. Despite her trademark silliness,
she was the first woman to run a production studio in

[50] http://quoteseed.com/quotes/anonymous/anonymous-being-both-soft-and-strong-is-a/

Hollywood. If you are a woman, use a Velvet Glove...feminine but firm. It works!

From the beginning of my career, I always used the Velvet Glove approach. Fully aware that I was a woman operating in a man's world, I embraced being feminine but also stayed firm. I kept a mental log of funny stories about my escapades and that helped take ego out of situations. My Number One tactic was to be myself. People seemed to naturally trust me when I was consulting with them, and they trusted me more the longer we worked together.

My clients knew that I would get them the best deal I could with the underwriters. If I made a mistake, I would be the first to tell them. If some situation happened, they could call me and I'd give them 100 percent of my best effort to set things right.

I used the same Velvet Glove approach with the underwriters. They trusted that I would not give them a "pig in a poke" by misrepresenting the risk. As a result, they were much more amenable in giving me favorable pricing and terms.

As you can imagine, we used a lot of humor in our company. McKenna used to say that I would "eat my young" (meaning, I'm overly aggressive). Well, I do have three kids...kidding!

Catch More Flies with Honey

As brokers, our job was to represent our clients in the insurance marketplace to secure coverage on their behalf. Brokers typically had a less-than positive reputation as far as ethics and for how they treated representatives and underwriters.

In the 1990s, Union Mutual Life Insurance (UNUM) held a major share of the physician Long Term Disability (LTD) market. Few carriers would assume the risk. If they did, they put significant limits on the coverage. UNUM did not. It was important for me to have a good relationship with their underwriters since a significant part of my book of business was physicians.

An Account Representative at UNUM mentioned that I would be surprised about how other brokers treat the underwriters. She said they liked me because I treated them with respect. In the insurance industry (and many others), setting yourself apart by having integrity will take you far.

Later, I had a significant renewal for one of my largest clients. When she presented their updates to me, I was not happy about the increase. I asked her to go back and hold the current rate. My Velvet Glove approach was successful in getting UNUM to hold the rate for another year.

Treat others the way that you want to be treated.

When the Velvet Glove Meets a Hammer

Speaking of eating your young, the movie *The Devil Wears Prada* has a scene where Miranda Priestly (the heartless editor) comes to work early, catching everyone off guard. Employees began calling their friends to warn them. Nigel (Director of Wardrobes) walked into a room and said, "All right, people, gird your loins."

I had experience with that kind of woman.

When working with accounts for a long time, inevitably your contact within the company will turnover. This happened at Friendly Hills Healthcare Network when Gloria Mayer replaced my contact, Tom McCabe.

During my first meeting with Gloria, she told me, "You should be fired!"

I sat there, stunned. I looked around to make sure she wasn't speaking to someone else. No one had ever said that to me before. While my approach in business was with that of a

Velvet Glove, Gloria preferred to use a hammer (actually more like an ax!)

I continued to work with her. Later, I came up with the Retention-Only concept while working on her account. Once that deal came through, I gave Gloria the credit for being the first group to implement it. This is really important: always make your client look good!

"Always make your client look good!"

I can't stress that enough. This is a perfect example. While we're at it: always make your boss look good! We'll come back to this later.

Gloria Mayer ended up being one of my biggest fans. She eventually became president of Friendly Hills Healthcare Network (FHHN) in La Habra, California. In 2000, she asked me to be a Board Member for FHHN, a $40-million-dollar non-profit organization that provided free healthcare services for underprivileged children in La Habra.

In another instance, during my time with Huntington Medical Group (HMG), the COO also turned over. While I don't remember her name, I do remember she was completely rude to me in our first meeting. Again, she used the hammer.

I went back to my office and thought about it for a few days. I finally put together a letter for the CEO and told him that I would, respectfully, not continue to provide consulting services for HMG. In essence, I was saying, "You're fired!"

The Velvet part was the letter to him saying that I would respectfully bow out. The Glove part: my decision was non-negotiable. I would not work with her.

Now, I wouldn't recommend you "try this at home" unless you have a lot of other business. He called me immediately to say he would remove her from working with us. I could work with him directly. That worked!

Because I was young, sometimes other employees in my own company would try to overpower me. Shortly after I moved over to the WF Corroon consulting division, working in business development, I had a meeting to pitch the Mullikin account. Mullikin Medical Centers was the largest Group in California. I brought our Human Resources Consultant Ginny Burdick with me.

In 1994, Mullikin delivered around $150,000 in commission income ($250,000 in today's dollars). I proposed that we deposit their commission into a "bank" they could use for whatever services we could provide, such as helping change their Human Resource policies, create benchmarking for salaries, provide retirement consulting, etc. I figured the bank concept would let us provide value-added services to tie ourselves in with them.

The "commission bank" approach gave us an edge over our competition. Traditional brokers could not compete against the services a consulting firm can provide.

Rebating insurance commissions was illegal in California, so providing service for commissions was a legal way to circumvent the California restriction. Once again, careful strategy.

After we landed the account, Ginny and I were in the parking lot, and she said that we shouldn't call ourselves brokers. We should call ourselves consultants.

The hair on the back of my neck went up as my internal alarms went off. I had brought my book of business from the Corroon and Black Division, and she was out-of-the-gates telling me what to do.

Another Velvet Glove example, I did not have a confrontation with her in the parking lot (Velvet). However, the next time I was in the office, I paid a visit to Manager Rick Mayo.

I sat down and said, "Does Ginny have any power in our division?"

He looked up from his computer screen. "Why?"

"Because I will not work with her going forward." (Glove).

Basically, this was my me-or-her ultimatum. When I told him why, he immediately said that she would be removed from any assignments that related to me.

As Miranda Priestly would say, "That's all."

Moral of the story: When you think you've been fired, don't give up. That person could end up being your biggest supporter!

Oh, and if you encounter a woman who uses a hammer approach, "Gird your loins, people!"

Vote with Your Feet

I did not encounter much sexism during my career. However, in 1989 a CEO gave it a shot. My book of business was getting larger, so I set a meeting with the CEO to discuss an increase in salary. When I told him what I wanted, he said, "How much do you and your husband need to make?"

I choked for a moment. Whenever someone blindsides you in a conversation, it's OK to pause. I had already heard about the comment, "She's a woman, how can she be worth it," but I'd never had someone try to put me in my place to my face.

I counted to three slowly in my head. My mind was firing off so many thoughts, I had to process them for a moment. I had that "You're the little woman" vibe coming at me, sort of like when I was in the South and they called me Honey with that "now go get us some coffee" feeling.

Careful to keep my tone calm and kind, I said, "This isn't about my husband. It's about my worth in the industry."

When breaking through barriers, we have to overcome multiple obstacles. Yes, it's challenging, and it feels like an uphill battle, but every gain is worth it.

I wasn't a partner, so I could vote with my feet (walk away with my book of business).

Also, there is a saying, "Don't mistake my kindness for weakness." That's really just another way to say Velvet Glove. Because I was nice and a woman, that CEO tried to work me. He had never met or worked with me before, so he figured he would be successful in convincing me that I didn't need that much money.

"Don't mistake my kindness for weakness."

He would have never opened that conversation with a man requesting an increase. Since he didn't want me to leave the company, he gave me what I asked for. All he needed was a tap with the velvet glove!

And, by the way, that never happened to me again.

Circa 1931 LOTTA AND MY DAD

"She gave the first breath of life to him 85 years ago. He reunited her grandchildren through the gift of his artwork."

THE ALLISON HERITAGE:

Breath of Life—My Dad and Lotta

When I was growing up, our house was full of books—books on shelves, books on tables, and books on fireplace mantles. None of them interested me...except one. The name was so unusual, I would turn my head sideways to read the title: *The Prophet* by Kahlil Gibran.

Kahlil Gibran was born in 1883 in Bsharri, Lebanon. *The Prophet* was Biblically inspired and especially popular in the 1960s. Historian Juan Cole said, "Many people turned away from the establishment of the Church to Gibran."[51]

Gibran offered a dogma-free universal spiritualism as opposed to Orthodox religion, and his perspective on the spiritual was not moralistic. In fact, he urged people to be non-judgmental. Now, I see why my parents were drawn to the book.

An excerpt from *The Prophet*:

Your joy is your sorrow unmasked.... the deeper
that sorrow carves into your being, the more joy
you can contain... when you are joyous, look
deep into your heart and you will find that it is
only that which has given you sorrow that is giving you joy.[52]

Breath of Life

My father was a joyous person who laughed a lot and loved people. His family and friends brought him joy. Despite the death of both parents when he was young, his brother's early

---

[51] Juan Cole, "Kahlil Gibran's The Prophet: Why was it so loved?" BBC News (BBC.com May 12, 2012)

[52] Kahlil Gibran, *The Prophet*, (New York: Knopf, 1923).

death and my sister's suicide, Dad still managed to stay positive. He had a light inside him that colored everything he did.

In the summer of 2014, my daughter, Jamie, took care of my dad during his last summer with us. He would regularly play "Rhapsody in Blue" on a boom box as it was his favorite piece of music. In July, while she was preparing to go back to school, Jamie chose her tryout song for Miami University to be "Breath of Life" (performed by Florence and the Machine from the movie, *Snow White and the Huntsman*).

Curious about her choice, I watched *Snow White and the Huntsman* and felt the powerful connection. That moment stayed with me.

After my dad passed on March 15, 2015, my cousin, Teresa, from New Mexico called me. She was coming to California in August and wanted to visit the Allison estate in La Jolla. My dad had always wanted me to go there, but I had never found the time, so I said, "Sure."

My dad's presence was with us that warm August day when Teresa and I set out on our adventure. Dad's boyhood home is now a historical landmark, one of the first houses on the top of the hill in La Jolla. It originally had horse stables, a tennis court, a pool, a guest house and the nine-room main house. Although the owners lived there, they were happy to show us around.

Dad had visited them twice. The second time, the owner figured out he was from the history of the house, and they became friends. She immediately remembered him when I told her who we were as we stood talking. Looking around, I could imagine my dad playing in these rooms, trying to escape his governess and talking to his mother, Lotta.

Teresa and I had a great time looking at the house. On the way home, I had a powerful impulse to write vignettes of family stories with my dad's art as the centerpiece. At the time, I had no idea those writings would become the foundation for this volume.

That same month, Miami University chose "Breath of Life" for their Short Program music during Jamie's senior year. The song title had come up twice in one year, and I felt curious to know why. I sat down one night and watched *Snow White and the Huntsman* again. The lightbulb went on in my mind. It had to do with my grandmother, Lotta Belle Snow, born 1895.

I wrote the following on dad's birthday, Tuesday September 8, 2015:

> I love the movie *Snow White and the Huntsman*. I find myself drawn to it. The special effects are fabulous with Charlize Theron as the evil Queen. However, Snow White captures my attention. Played by Kristen Stewart, she is the heroine who comes into her rightful role as Queen with courage, strength, resolve, and most of all, heart. The movie's signature song, "Breath of Life," elicits the battle scene where she fearlessly leads an inspired people and their army to seize her birthright role as Queen.
>
> Just as Snow White had courage, strength, resolve, and most of all heart, so did my grandmother Carlotta (Lotta). Yesterday, in my dad's baby book I came across a picture of Lotta in Hawaii. Today, he would be 85.

Lotta had a passion for teaching. In 1917, when she was twenty-two, she went beyond California all the way to the Hawaiian Islands to teach. Lotta had courage and strength to venture all the way across the Pacific Ocean with two friends.

This adventurous spirit was in her blood. She was a descendant of Richard Snow of Woburn who came to America on one of the Great Immigration Ships called *Expedition* in 1635. Her father, Edwin Wheelock Snow had a sense of humor and named his little girl, Lotta Snow (a lot of snow). She did not share his humor and later changed her name to Carlotta.

Circa 1917 Lotta on the Big Island of Hawaii

Meanwhile, my grandfather was Chief Engineer. Part of his job was to maintain and protect the interests of the Imperial Irrigation District across the border in Mexico. For many years during the Mexican Revolution, their water supply was a target of rebel factions. Whenever a rebel attack occurred, J.C. would check the water supply to make sure it was intact. He would then report it to General Holabird who would communicate with Washington D.C.

In the early 1920s, J.C. attended a dinner at the home of a business associate. Freshly back in the U.S. after her Hawaiian adventure, Lotta also received an invitation for dinner. She was a friend of the man's wife.

What some might call a coincidence was actually destiny.

It was love at first sight. They were married about a year later.

In 1922, J.C. and Lotta sailed to Japan where J.C. was negotiating Foreign Trade with Japanese dignitaries. While he was in a diplomatic meeting, Lotta wrote in her diary:

Oct. 18, 1922. Wednesday – Chester went to a luncheon at Mr. Asano's. It is raining and quite gloomy. I feel lonely and wish C. were with me now. I can't bear to be away from him."

When J.C. returned, he wrote, "I love you, Lotta," underneath her journal entry.

Several years passed. They had two children, Joan and Ned, and moved into the house in La Jolla.

From left: J.C. and Lotta; Allison Estate circa 1920s and 2015;
Joan, Lotta and Ned

Lotta became pregnant a third time, this time with my father. Back then, they did not have technology that allowed a peek at the gender before birth, so they had one girl's name picked out, Diane Gould Allison, and a slew of boy's names picked out.

My dad took his first breath of life on September 8, 1930, at 12:50 (no am/pm designation). They named him Gould. With a name like Gould, there was no need for a middle name. He had golden locks, so they affectionately called him Gouldie locks.

For the next six years, J.C., Lotta and their three children lived an idyllic life on Hillside Drive in La Jolla.

In 1936, Lotta became a widow to raise her three children alone. The robbery left her with J.C.'s complicated affairs to sort out. Unfortunately, she had no idea how to manage the finances and ended up losing the family home when it was sold for back taxes.

When my dad was twelve, he was playing on a white picket fence and fell. The fence impaled his spleen. Lotta rushed him to Scripps Memorial Hospital in La Jolla, the same hospital where she gave birth to him. The doctors did not expect him to pull through.

Lotta was devastated. She visited him in the hospital every day, and each day she would bring a poem she had hand-written and read it to him.

On June 2, 1942, Lotta put the Tuesday poem in her purse and headed toward La Jolla to visit my dad.

Tuesday poem
My boy is the light
In the sky
As a soft light comes
gently through my window
at break of day.
My boy is the star at
night in a velvet sky.
He is the breeze coming nearer, nearer and gayley
whispering to me.
Life is beautiful with him
by my side.

And life has meaning for
he is with me.
And near me always

On the way to the hospital, she was in a horrific car accident where her car was sandwiched between two military trucks. The ambulance brought her to Scripps. At age forty-seven, Lotta took her last breath of life two floors below my dad's hospital bed.

The doctors felt it best not to tell my dad of Lotta's passing, so he would have a better chance to recover. Even his sixth-grade class who visited at the hospital didn't say a word about what happened.

When Lotta's life came to an end, so did the family unit. Different family members took the three siblings, and they grew up apart.

Lotta is the heroine of the Allison story. She was a woman with strength, courage and resolve, but most importantly a woman who led with her heart.

Continuing my vignette from September 8, 2015:
Today is Tuesday. My dad is with her again. I can't help but think that she is happy and proud of him. She gave the first breath of life to him 85 years ago. He reunited her grandchildren through the gift of his artwork.

"She gave him his first breath of life 85 years ago...she took her last breath of life two floors below him."

In 2015, for the first time in the history of their program Jamie's team debut was moved from Ann Arbor, Michigan, to Anaheim, California—to the very same rink where Jamie competed when she was younger and where Michael clinched the Crosstown Cup over rival USC. Anaheim ICE was a place where our family gathered to watch many competitions over the years. The day of Jamie's competition, I felt my dad there with us again.

LEFT: Michael and me at Anaheim Ice 2013 CENTER: Jamie center with her team debut, Anaheim Ice 2015 RIGHT: My dad with Michael at Anaheim Ice 2011

Miami University (Team USA 2) went on to the 2016 World Championships in Budapest, Hungary finishing 8th overall out of 25 teams.

"I was looking for a Breath of Life, for a little touch of heavenly light, to get a dream of life again, a little vision of the start and the end, and if you are gone, I will not belong here, but the room is so quiet, oh oh oh ooh."

To watch Jamie and her team compete, go to YouTube:
Spring Cup 2016 - Miami University - Short Program
Music: "Breath of Life" by Florence and the Machine
https://www.youtube.com/watch?v=9u_BPfuLb2s

Mentoring Jamie

When Jamie made the California Gold team, she was the youngest on the team as the age range was 14 to 26. The team had just earned a Fourth-Place finish at National's, so measuring up to veteran team members was not easy for her. Eleven returning skaters had medaled. In a sense, some team members felt that Jamie had not paid her dues: first, because she was a newcomer and, second, she was only 14.

She didn't let her teammates' attitude stop her. She consistently asked her coach what she had to do to earn a spot on the ice. She wasn't shy, but she had to walk a bit of a tightrope and not alienate the returning skaters. This was all intuitive for her as we never had any discussions about her approach.

She worked hard to deliver what the coach wanted. When she finally got a spot, her coach used her drive as an example, saying that Jamie showed how much she wanted it and did what it took to get it.

The first time she skated at National's was in 2009, and then she went on to skate internationally. She was a freshman in high school.

Synchronized skating epitomizes the concept of the Velvet Glove. On the ice, the skaters are a balance of grace and beauty while exhibiting tremendous strength as they skate their program and complete their lifts. These girls can be a prom queen or a tom boy, whatever the situation calls for.

The Glove part: Jamie spoke up for herself, just as I had to do on so many occasions throughout my career. The Velvet part: understand group politics, so you can be more likable to the veteran skaters.

She aimed high and refused the no.

When you know your worth and speak up for it, the combination of strong and soft as a woman will take you far in your life and career.

"When you know your worth and speak up for it, the combination of strong and soft as a woman will take you far in your life and career."

2009 Jamie and Tori at the Spring Cup in Milan, Italy

In 2009, California Gold competed in the Spring Cup in Milan, Italy, and earned a silver medal for the USA.
To watch Jamie and team compete at the Spring Cup, go to YouTube:

To view this Go to YouTube:
Spring Cup 2009 -California Gold - USA - Senior FP:
https://www.youtube.com/watch?v=0VLnIOjTxmg

A LUCY MOMENT
Napoli and the One-Eyed Driver

They're gonna put me in the movies, they're gonna make a big star out of me. They're gonna put me in the movies and all I gotta do is act naturally. ~The Beatles

In 2009, I attended Jamie's Team USA competition at the Spring Cup in Milan with Tori's father, John, and Tori who was three at the time. While I was retired from my career, I was not retired from traveling for Jamie's competitions. All those years, I tried to blame my Lucy Moments on work, but, apparently, I am the common denominator.

After the competition, we traveled south to Napoli via train. Our plan was to end up in Positano, a beautiful cliffside city on the Amalfi Coast of Italy. We took the train as far as it went before we had to find other transportation through the cliff sides to Positano.

Napoli's Mafia is one of four major criminal networks currently in Italy (along with Sicily, of course). Of course, it was my idea to get off there. We quickly discovered that it was not a safe place for a couple and a small child to be stranded. What was I thinking!

We got off the train in Napoli. When we walked out of the train station, no taxis were in sight, just guys standing around talking to each other. It was getting late, so John told me to wait on a corner while he went to talk to the guys to see if he could find a taxi.

Meanwhile, I stood there with three-year-old Tori in a stroller, my vivid imagination already stirring up scenarios about someone trying to take her. I had two thoughts: *Why me?* and *How am I going to get out of this one!*

When John finally returned, he said the guys told him someone named Mario would drive us to Positano. Mario came out from the back of the group, as if he was the bottom of the barrel. I'm thinking, *Phew!*

We dropped our things into his car, jumped in and off we went. This car was not a taxi. It was a private car. Mario set off driving like a bat out of hell, like Italian cab drivers do. After forty-five minutes of driving on a cliff highway, we were taking the high road…literally.

After a while, I noticed that Mario had one eye like Marty Feldman in Young Frankenstein. The cliff was on the right, but his good eye was on the left. Mario didn't seem to notice. He didn't let a little thing like a missing eye slow him down.

John and I were speechless. I gave him the wide-eyed Lucy look.

We finally made it to Positano at 9 p.m. For the rest of our stay, we took a bus or we walked. No more cabs for us that entire trip!

CHAPTER 9

Wear Your Selling Suit

Self Confidence is the best outfit. Rock it, and own it.[53] ~Confident Designs

When you have an appointment to pitch an account or deliver a presentation to executive Board members, wear your selling suit. You know, that special outfit that makes you feel great, that makes you feel like, I've got this. Lay out your outfit the night before, and check your shoes.

---

[53] Confident Designs, August 21, 2019.

Wear your selling suit, and check your shoes.

After I landed the Friendly Hills account, Dr. Barnett referred me to the California Primary Physician Medical Group in downtown Los Angeles. At that point, I knew I was onto something with going after the medical groups. I also figured out that I was a closer, and I started paying attention to every detail of my delivery.

In order to close a deal, you need full 100 percent confidence that you will succeed.

1997 Michael, Jamie and me in one of my favorite selling suits

Confidence includes your appearance. That is when I came up with the selling-suit concept. When I looked like a million dollars, I could earn millions for the company.

"In order to close a deal, you need full 100 percent confidence that you will succeed."

One of my first selling suits was the cream suit in the picture above. I would wear cream shoes, colorful blouses and pearls, always pearls. All of the guys wore power suits with expensive cufflinks, so I wore my feminine power suit. Like Reese Witherspoon when she became an attorney, she still wore feminine clothes but packed a punch with her delivery and charm.

When I did business with Lloyd's of London in the 1990s, I definitely wore my selling suit. I was playing to win. I was playing for keeps. Only this time, the game was on an international scale where today they trade $50 Billion dollars of coverage annually.

In 1997, I flew to London to meet with Lloyd's underwriters to discuss emerging risks in California. The Lloyd's building is iconic steel with glass elevators on the outside, offering an amazing view over London. On weekdays, the building is filled with power suits while brokers convince some of the best underwriters in the world to take a particular risk that other insurance carriers are not yet ready to consider.

While the building shouts ultra-modern, a traditional doorman in a red coat greets everyone passing. Once inside the building, guests register to go on a tour, since Lloyd's of London is not open to the public. Representing both new and old, this is where modern business and history intersect.

As we toured, the underwriting floor felt comfortable to me, oddly familiar. We passed a portrait of Winston Churchill sitting on a chair under an oak tree. It captured my attention. I had to pull myself away.

Churchill served as the First Lord of the Admiralty and political head of the Royal Navy during the second World

War. If the Allied navies ended the Battle of the Atlantic in defeat, the cost of the compensation would have bankrupted Lloyd's. In very real ways, Lloyd's owes Winston Churchill a debt of gratitude.

Lloyd's of London - left, exterior; right, interior

Unbeknownst to me at the time, J.C. Allison's mother, my great-grandmother Mary Churchill had an ancestral link to the Churchill's of Devonshire, England. Circa 1500, I had common ancestors with Sir Winston Churchill and Princess Diana. About 350 years after my ancestors left England, I stepped into Lloyd's at the height of my career and came full circle with my British heritage.

At that point in my career, at least once a year we would bring some of the leading CEO's of managed care to sit down with the underwriters. Because risk was shifting from the insurance companies to the providers, new opportunities were opening. Lloyd's of London is known for underwriting unusual or emerging risks

First of all, unlike domestic carriers, Lloyd's will only conduct business face to face. Working with Lloyd's underwriters, I learned that during a negotiation, the moment he or she starts to write something, stop talking. You have convinced them to take the risk, now it is time to shut up. This is true in general. When someone starts sending buying signals, don't talk yourself out of a sale.

Don't talk yourself out of a sale.

California was the frontier for managed care. For the first time, physicians were taking the risk for their patients. This model moved East from there. The two women that I accompanied on the trip represented two of the largest managed care populations in the country: Scripps Clinic in San Diego and Friendly Hills Healthcare Network in La Habra. At that time, women seldom occupied top positions in the healthcare industry, the same as women seldom occupied top positions in brokerage companies. Times were changing.

We three female executives entered Lloyd's of London to educate the underwriters on what was happening in healthcare in California. A new era had arrived, and female executives were leading the way. What's even more unusual was that Myrna Merritt, our underwriter at Lloyd's, was a woman. Myrna was tough, intelligent and well respected.

"A new era had arrived, and female executives were leading the way."

I had been to London many times before as Lloyd's of London insured many of our clients for capitation stop-loss. Because of my partner, Jerry Sullivan, I was allowed in the underwriting room in the 1990s when the brokers were 90 percent male, with automatic respect.

Lloyd's market has been at the forefront of its industry for more than 300 years, pioneering new forms of protection for a changing world. Lloyd's is not an insurance company per se, but a group of 99 syndicates, or investment groups, with a common interest. These members price and underwrite policies and spread the risk amongst themselves.

With Gloria Mayer, we were at dinner at The Cavalry and Guard's Club, established in 1810. The members were traditionally the most socially elite of the British Army. We had Beef Wellington in the Duke of Wellington Room (of course!). The Duke of Wellington was a great military leader and Prime Minister. I have an ancestral link with the 1st Duke of Marlborough (John Churchill). A century earlier, he would have been a member as he was one of the most famous British Generals of the 18th century.

Special members called Names are high net-worth individuals who underwrite risks with unlimited exposure. The Names were often referred to as those individuals who could lose everything "down to the cuff links" (i.e.: the shirt off their backs). Over the years, the amount of risk that the Names take has since been limited.

Jerry Sullivan's father was one of the first American correspondents with Lloyd's of London. Jerry formed his own relationship with Lloyd's and is considered a significant supporter to this day. As a result, Jerry was treated like royalty. Becoming partners with Jerry opened the door for me at Lloyd's.

**"Becoming partners with Jerry opened the
door for me at Lloyd's."**

In London, Jerry's driver in a black Daimler would take
us wherever we needed to go. We were very spoiled. So spoiled,
that any other time I traveled to Europe, as I left a building, I
would look for my driver. Then it would sink in that I was no
longer with Sullivan!

Sullivan put together an exclusive joint venture between
Farmer and Lloyd's in the 1970s and '80s. He pioneered the first
"structured settlement" policy, and Frank McKenna pioneered the
first capitation stop-loss contract. Jerry Sullivan and his father
along with Frank McKenna made up three generations of insurance pioneers, three generations of history with Lloyd's of London.

Sullivan and McKenna had such a degree of trust with
Lloyd's that they would do business on a handshake. They
could literally draw up a scheme on a cocktail napkin, and a
whole new kind of coverage would be born. Sullivan and
McKenna were brilliant. The underwriters were the best in the
world. I was in the inner sanctum of insurance and, at the time,
I didn't even realize it.

**"I was in the inner sanctum of insurance and,
at the time, I didn't even realize it."**

When I would wear my selling suit, McKenna would
wear his as well. In some cases, his cufflinks cost as much as his
custom-tailored suit. He had his suits made by a tailor who
would come to our offices.

Feeling left out, one day I asked the tailor if he made
women's suits and he said, "Of course!" So, I had my suits made,
too…in feminine colors.

Joyce Reynolds, Gloria Mayer and me.

"A new era had arrived...
female executives were
leading the way."

THE ALLISON HERITAGE:

Lloyd's of London and Churchill

Many famous people have a signature style. Sir Elton John wore oversized glasses. Audrey Hepburn had her black dress and pearls, and Sir Winston Churchill had his top hats. Those top hats were his selling suit.

He once wrote a humorous essay remarking that as he did not have a distinctive hairstyle, spectacles, or facial hair like other famous statesmen, so the press focused on his headgear. The Homburg felt hat was his favorite. In 1991, one of his favorite hats sold at auction for $11,750.

My dad and I were always fascinated by any movies or TV shows that had to do with the British Monarchy. When he was young, Dad sketched a beautiful English manor he called Brimpton. I'm curious where he got the idea for it. Perhaps his family told him stories.

When I was growing up in La Canada, Dad always mentioned that we were related to Winston Churchill. He just couldn't prove it.

He left me a file named "Churchill" and I finally did the research.

Our namesake ancestor, Josiah Churchill, sailed to Connecticut from England in the 1630s. Josiah has a Y DNA match to the Devonshire (Winston/Spencer) Churchills. He also is the only Churchill in the American Colonies who has a match with Gitto/Otho Leon, a Norman Knight circa 960 who is at the top of the Churchill lineage. The Churchill ancestral tree includes John Churchill, who was the 1st Duke of Marlborough, Winston Churchill, Princess Diana and Prince William, the future King of England.

In 1940, Prime Minister Churchill, gave a speech at the beginning of World War II to boost British morale. "Their Finest Hour" was one of the most famous speeches of all time. Winston Churchill is considered one of the best war strategists in history. He came by it honestly and studied his ancestor John Churchill. By assimilating John Churchill's methods, Winston Churchill led Britain to victory against Adolf Hitler.

Be True to You

Along with his exemplary leadership, Churchill had a hallmark of being honest and transparent, both personally and professionally. When you are honest, people trust you. That is the best way to lead.

1997 DIANA "Candle in the Wind" My dad's commemoration of Princess Diana's memorial service on September 6, 1997. Elton John sang, "A Candle in the Wind." Go to Youtube and search: **Lady Diana - Candle in the wind (Goodbye England's Rose) - Elton John - Lyrics in text**
https://www.youtube.com/watch?v=OefdqK3jKi0&t=117s

Mentoring Michael

Every year, when Michael and his friends came home for the holidays, they would get together to play a board game called Axis and Allies, a strategy game about World War II.

Michael graduated from UCLA in Economics, AJ graduated from Berkeley in Business, and Apoorva is finishing his residency to become a doctor graduating from USC. You could say they are a bit of a think tank.

The game was always sprawled across my dining room table. They played it over a period of two days, on and off for twelve hours at a time.

Don't leave money on the table.

I never mentored Michael in the art of strategy, but we did have a running contest going. Whenever money was part of our conversation, neither of us wanted to throw out the first number. We'd parlay for hours, waiting for the other one to give in and say a number. Although I never gave Michael a lesson in strategy, we did quite a bit of hands-on practice. And, it probably didn't hurt that our lineage is known for it.

Strategy was my favorite part of business. I'd figure out which carriers were aligned with my competitors and which clients were aligned with which competitors. Then I'd come up with a play to close the deal...and, yes, I always wore my selling suit.

Business is one big chess game. As with any game, you win more often if strategy is your strong suit.

A LUCY MOMENT

Wear Your Selling Suit, and Don't Stab Your Crouton

The morning I was giving a presentation in front of the Board of Directors for Unified Medical Group Association, I was running late and dressed in a hurry. The top CEO's of the biggest groups in Southern California would be at that meeting.

I was presenting a benefits survey they could use to benchmark their own Group's plans. My graphs and presentation materials looked good, and I looked good. I felt at the top of my game that day.

In the middle of the presentation, I glanced down at my shoes. They were two different colors: one black, one blue. At least they were the same style. I have a habit of buying more than one color of something when I like it.

The tables in front of me formed a square horseshoe. I was front and center with nowhere to hide. *Did anyone notice?* I finished the presentation like nothing was wrong.

As we walked out of the room, Diane Bailey the Human Resources Director was beside me. I couldn't hold it in any longer. I said, "Diane, did you notice I have on different colored shoes?"

She laughed and said, "No."

At lunch with the executives, I ordered a salad with ranch dressing. I went to stab a crouton and it flung on the CEO next to me. My face was on fire. He laughed as he wiped ranch dressing off of his tailored Italian suit.

That time, I wasn't laughing.

People would often say, "I can't believe that happened to you!" when I shared one of my escapades.

I would retort, "Try being me!"

My colleagues and close clients would laugh every time I said that...but I was serious!

Honestly, try being me when you think you are going in for a crouton and it flings on the CEO next to you. I was wearing my selling suit and wanted to leave an impression on that room full of prospects. Well, I left an impression, all right. Just not the one I intended!

I always had a habit of laying out my outfit the night before, but after that I also included my shoes.

Wear your selling suit, and check your shoes. Also, when eating a salad at a table filled with executives, scoop your crouton. Do not stab.

CHAPTER 10

Humor: The Winning Edge

If I were two faced, would I be wearing this one?[54]
~Abraham Lincoln

Humor is currency. Self-deprecation is even better. I learned it from my father. When a situation is intense, the best way to break the ice or defuse the tension is to make fun of yourself. Abraham Lincoln was a master at it with his many stories. Here is one of my favorites, paraphrased from *Lincoln's Yarns and Stories,* by Alexander K. McClure.

---

[54] https://www.brainyquote.com/quotes/abraham_lincoln_103534

One day, a scowling man drew a revolver and aimed it inches from Lincoln's face.

Shocked, Lincoln said, "What's the matter?"

The stranger replied, "I swore an oath that if I ever came across an uglier man than myself, I'd shoot him on the spot."

Lincoln merely smiled. "Shoot me," he said. "If I'm uglier than you, I don't want to live."[55]

A fan of Shakespeare, Lincoln's wit served him well. He combined reflection with self-deprecation, a combination that Shakespeare used extensively. It worked for Shakespeare. It worked for Lincoln... and it worked for me.

When someone in our group had this gift of humor, I became a straight man and set them up to go in for the kill with the punchline and get the laughs. My partners and friends knew this, so I always teased them that I made them look good.

We would laugh, and they would say that any self-respecting person would seize the opportunity to close the joke at my expense. I may have been the butt of the jokes, but I laughed all of the way to the bank.

People love humor. It is currency.

"I may have been the butt of the jokes, but I laughed all of the way to the bank."

Where Do Your Parents Live?

In 1998, I started looking for a house in Huntington Beach. My realtor showed me one house that didn't do it for me, and nothing more. As usual, I took action and found a newspaper advertisement that showed a house with sand in

---

[55] Alexander K. McClure, *Lincoln's Yarns and Stories*, (Project Gutenberg: Release Date: February, 2001 [E-Book #2517] Last Updated: November 15, 2016) https://www.gutenberg.org/files/2517/2517-h/2517-h.htm#link2H_4_0018

the back. I clipped it out and gave it to the realtor, asking him to take me there. The price was listed at $997,000 ($1.6 million today).

Just one look, and I was in love.

The house and the property had everything I wanted. It was kind of Cape-Cod-esque for the kids to grow up in. It would be great for family gatherings and perfect for entertaining clients.

What a quantum leap from my growing up in a 1,300-square-foot house with three girls sharing a room and a bathroom with zero water pressure. My dream house was 3,200 square feet with three bedrooms and three baths, and a backyard with a beach.

It also had a thirty-six-foot dock in a marina around the corner. In Coral Cay, there were two boating options: If you buy on the sand, your dock is thirty-six-feet long in the marina. If you buy on the deep-water side, your dock is forty feet long or greater, and it is in your back yard. I chose the sand side because I had children and the deep side terrified me. What if they fell in? Besides, any boat bigger than a twelve-foot Duffy would spell Lucy-trouble for me.

We moved into our dream house in May. The first party I gave was a Christmas party to watch the boat parade for some of the most influential healthcare executives in Southern California. I called the event "Christmas on the Cay," since cay means cove. The invitation was in a box with a clear sailboat as an ornament keepsake.

In La Canada, if you lived below Foothill Boulevard, you were probably wealthy. If you lived above the boulevard, you were middle class. We now lived below the boulevard.

"We now lived below the boulevard."

This neighborhood was the elite part of Huntington Harbor. Coral Cay residents were generally entrepreneurs with

family-owned companies. Their houses were kept in the family.
Grown children would live in the family home when the parents
passed off the scene.

1998 TOP LEFT: Coral Cay TOP RIGHT: Michael and Jamie in our backyard BELOW: Christmas Party set-up

The founder of Grey Goose lived around the corner from
me. The founder of Lee Press On Nails lived down the street
with her 110-foot yacht moored to her corner dock. Michael
would often fish off of her dock. My next-door neighbor was a
founder of a staffing company that sold during the tech boom for
$150 million.

Then there was me.

More times than I can count, people assumed that because I was a woman, I made my money from a divorce. I attended my first Homeowners Association meeting in the Huntington Harbor Yacht Club. I walked in to find the room filled with octogenarians (some with walkers and some with oxygen).

Wanting to be polite, I took a chair quietly and said hello to the gentleman with the oxygen tank next to me. He nodded and returned the greeting. Someone from the Board of Directors passed out a sign in sheet, and the meeting officially came to order.

Immediately, the president looked at me and asked me to introduce myself. I did.

His first question: "Where do your parents live?"

I hesitated and glanced around to make sure he was talking to me. "I'm a homeowner," I said.

He did a double take, like he was checking for a second head.

This happened to me again and again. I was thirty-eight years old, a single woman with two small children who had made my own way and purchased my own house. They just didn't know what to do with me.

My grandfather bought a house on a La Jolla hilltop, and I bought one on the beach. We both had the same goal: entertaining clients. Remember, people do business with people they like. The more real you are, the more apt they will be to give you their business.

"The more real you are, the more apt they will be to give you their business."

People do business with people they like.

J.C. and Lotta in Japan

Characteristics of business people I not only liked, but I looked up to include:

1. They are funny. Humor gets my attention every time.

2. They are real and not afraid to show their flaws.

3. They are interested in everyone and not pretentious.

4. They care about their encounter with me and show it by putting away their phones.

5. They are genuinely interested and ask questions to get to know me. They are not arrogant.

6. They give praise and take blame. When congratulated about an achievement, they thank their team. When something bad happens, they assume the blame for their team.

Lotta and J.C. sail to Japan.

"I love a ship and it's smells,
noises, rushing of passengers to find
their places is all very exciting..."
~Lotta Snow Allison

THE ALLISON HERITAGE:

J.C. and Japan Trade

In 2008, I called my dad and said, "I can't do it."

He said, "Do what?"

"I can't take care of you in La Canada and the kids in Huntington Beach. I need you to move here, so I can take care of both you and the kids."

I was ready for resistance. My dad was a glued fixture in La Canada. That's where he was an activist, where he raised us girls and where he was with my mom. I figured I was going to have to pry him out of there.

I was always looking out for my dad, but he was also looking out for me. Without hesitation, he agreed.

That same day, I found a realtor and listed his house. When it came time to pack up, he and I discussed his forty-seven years' worth of belongings—what would go with him and what would go into the dumpster.

I pulled the wooden Indian totem pole from the hallway and gave him a look.

He said, "Yes." That totem pole was legendary among my childhood friends. Everyone had to pass it on the way to my room, and it terrified those little girls. It was coming to Huntington Beach.

His painting, *The Girl in The Red Tights*, was an original painting of my sisters, my cousins and my Uncle Ned at the La Jolla tide pools. That went into my car, along with all of our family history files.

In 2013, two years before he passed, my dad handed me a small green book and a small brochure. "Keep this," he said.

I looked at it, curious. About the size of my hand, it looked ancient and worn.

1963 Photo of *The Girl in the Red Tights*

A few days later, I randomly opened it to the middle of the book... and went to a whole different world. My dad had handed me Lotta's diary from a trip to Japan in 1922 with my grandfather. From the first entry, I was hooked. She made me feel as if I were there.

Journal Entry

Friday, October 6, 1922

> Masquerade ball tonight. Had fun. Some costumes were fantastic, poorest music ever.... Mr. Nakamura's son is to be married. Mrs. N. is taking over part of new daughter's trousseau she let

me wear one of the kimonos. It was gray silk, the obi beautifully colored with a rich red.

First Mrs. N's maid put a short loose cotton kimono on me. Then she folded the gray kimono way around me and bound me with a flat cord around my waist about six times and pulled tightly, after fitting a little green silk regular corset. Then came the heavy stiff obi, about 1 ft wide. This was wrapped around waist about 2 times and an immense butterfly bow tied in back & fastened with more cord and pins.

Wore two chrysanthemums over my ears. I made them of red paper. She told me that j women of high caste never wear red in their hair. Mrs. N. & maid seemed pleased with the result. The j. men would clap when C. and I approached them.

Sunday, October 29, 1922

Passed some children, one little boy was dangling a small bird, tied by its wings to a string. Chester bought the bird for 10 sen. Poor little bird, one girl said it was called "Suzami." I warmed it in both my hands, carried it for two miles, it seemed much better, blinked its eyes, wrestled about a bit, and drank a little water. As we were going to go back over the trails off from the main road, I had to get a box for it. The poor little thing died before we went very far. I buried it above a small stone Buddha at the first bridge. We walked the entire 10 miles home.

Sunday, October 22, 1922

> Went past Big Hell just before it was real dark, could hear the water churning & boiling in the big crevice. The trail was fairly good from here on & we did some tall sprinting. All the other rest houses were closed. Wonderful place for a murder! No noise except of falling waterfall! Reached the cable car station at 2 min of 6. We were darned lucky, once more.

Saturday, November 3, 1922

> Chester and I went to a ball game...Chester and Heinie wore light suits, canes & gloves. Their sleeves didn't reach the gloves & I was disturbed, didn't care if Chester wanted to wear them that way but just thought I would say something quietly, for it really looked sort of funny. Said "Chester, you shouldn't wear gloves when your shirt cuff comes below your sleeves." He said, "Mind your own business & I'll mind mine."

> Right then, I wish I didn't love Chester quite so much as a cross word from him wouldn't hurt so much. If anyone else on earth had said that to me, I would have told them where to go... Chester didn't feel well that night. He told me he was sorry. I love him so I will forget about it all in a few days. I don't want him to talk to me like that, I am afraid of what might happen.

I put the journal away in a safe place. After I visited the Allison estate with my cousin in 2015, I took the diary out again. The thought occurred to me that my grandfather was probably working during the trip. If he was anything like me, he had to.

My grandfather had powers of persuasion and skills of diplomacy. People liked him. He was not only a developer of water resources, but he was also a major developer of foreign trade.

The second time I opened the diary, I looked closer at the dates and entries. On September 22, 1922, my grandparents sailed on the steamer ship *Shinyo Maru* to Hawaii and then to Japan.

As I read my grandmother's entire diary, I saw that my grandfather, J.C., had meetings at the Mexican Embassy and at the American Embassy with Viscount Shibusawa, dubbed the Father of Capitalism in Japan. J.C. also met with the future Prime Minister on that trip. His itinerary was a veritable Who's Who of Japanese nobility.

He also met with Baron Asano Soichiro, a shipping tycoon and owner of the steamer they traveled on. In the 1950s, a Broadway play, "A Majority of One," was based on the life of Baron Asano. The role of the Baron required an actor who could show "emotional tenderness and an Eastern sense of humor."[56]

The L.A. power structure was vested in my grandfather's trip to Japan. They were sending their best negotiator, J.C. Allison. Why else would General Moses H. Sherman see my grandparents off at the dock in San Francisco. Sherman was worth $150 million in today's dollars. Powerful men like that, do everything for a reason.

[56] T.H. McCulloh, "Majority Can't Rescue 'One'," *Los Angeles Times*, March 22,1995, p. OCF2.

Journal Entry

September 21, 1922

Had our picture taken, the whole party of us for some Japanese magazine.

General Sherman was smiling broadly and waving his hat as the boat pulled away from the dock.

We found a beautiful bouquet of flowers in our stateroom from General Sherman.

I love a ship and the smells, noises, rushing of passengers to find their places is all very exciting.

Monday, October 16, 1922
    Chester went to the American Embassy.

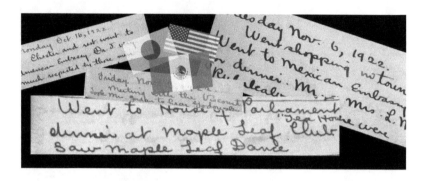

Friday, November 3, 1922
    Meeting with the Viscount.

1st Viscount Shibusawa Elichi – dubbed the
"Father of Japanese Capitalism."

In 2024, Elichi Shibusawa will be featured on the Y10,000 bill. Known for modernizing the Japanese economy.[57] He was a

---

[57] Reiji Yoshida, "Japan announces new Y10,000, Y5,000, Y1,000 bank notes as Reiwa Era looms," *The Japan Times*, April 9, 2019.

humanitarian and leader of Japan shown by his acceptance of Christian Armenian genocide refugees in 1922.

Wednesday, October 25th, 1922

"Road to luncheon given by Baron Shidehara, Ambassador to the U.S.A. at the Villa of Baron."

Baron Kijuro Shidehara – cover of Time Magazine, Oct. 12, 1931 JAPAN'S MAN OF PEACE AND WAR

In 1919, Shidehara was the Japanese Ambassador to the United States. He became Prime Minister Post-World War II due to his views on pacifism. He is the son-in-law of the founder of Mitsubishi.[58]

---

[58] "Kijuro Shidehara,"

Tuesday November 6, 1922
Went to Mexican Embassy for dinner...

Baron Asano Soichiro – Japanese businessman responsible for founding a
number of companies including what became today's Sapporo Breweries. In
addition, he owned Asano Shipping. My grandparents were on the Shinyo
Maru, one of his ships.[59]

When I looked at the brochure Dad gave me with Lotta's
diary, I saw a picture of Baron Asano and his wife as well as a picture of the Baron's Villa where J.C. and Lotta had tea. On the
back of the brochure was a picture of the ship my grandparents
sailed on.

The L.A. power structure wanted something. The
Japanese wanted something. My grandfather sailed to Japan to
be the closer.

"My grandfather sailed to Japan to be the closer."

To be in a powerful scenario like this, you have to not

---

      https://en.wikipedia.org/wiki/Kij%C5%ABr%C5%8D_Shidehara

[59] "Asano Soichiro,"
      https://en.wikipedia.org/wiki/Asano_S%C5%8Dichir%C5%8D

only be likeable, but you have to be trustworthy and have expertise. These are once-in-a-lifetime situations that only happen to a handful of people. My grandfather had to be on the top of his game.

Luck is where preparation meets opportunity.

So much was riding on J.C. that trip. Here's his checklist for success:
— Wear your selling suit.
— Make sure your shoes match.
— Don't order ranch.
— If ranch is your option, scoop your crouton!
— *Just kidding...*
The Real Checklist
J.C. had been preparing for this opportunity all his life. He was in the middle of the granddaddy of foreign trade deals. At the same time, humor makes the big deals seem normal. Humor also implies confidence.

I can.

My grandfather was successful in his negotiations. From the San Diego Tribune, May 29, 1936:
He recently returned from Mexico, D. F. and Central America, where he had arranged for the shipment of coffee and sugar through this port, commencing in the fall....
Through his trade development efforts, cargo went through the Port of San Diego which

previously had gone through other ports. He planned a large cotton production program, in which the Port of San Diego would benefit by shipments to Japan through here....

As a result of his securing accounts for shipments through this port, steamers from European ports arrived here with goods which had been imported by his firm for distribution throughout the southwest.[60]

After he constructed the water system to sustain agriculture, in 1924 my grandfather leased 100,000 acres in Baja California. He planted the entire 100,000 acres with cotton.

When the stock market crashed in 1928, the Allison Estate stayed profitable because of this cotton crop. For perspective on the size of this land area, if someone starts driving in Tijuana and heads north over the border past San Diego and La Jolla...past Laguna...past West Los Angeles...continuing for 2.5 hours...ending up in the San Fernando Valley—if you put that area into square miles, you'll have the amount of cotton my grandfather planted in Baja California.

Mentoring Michael and Jamie: Roughing Up the Cubs

Humor is the hallmark for our family. My dad's grandchildren are my sister's sons, Justin a mechanical engineer and Brandon a civil engineer, then my children, Michael a Principal in his company, Jamie with her Doctorate and up-and-coming Tori. Mix humor with all of that, and we are a collective family of smartasses.

When we get together, we stay up late telling stories about each other and laughing. We have no mercy. Our philosophy: If we like you, we tease you. The more we like you, the more we tease you.

---

[60] *San Diego Tribune*," J. C. Allison Civic Leader Is Dead," May 29, 1936.

Each one of us has been the brunt of many stories. In our family, you need to be able to dish it out, but most importantly, you need to be able to take it. We train them young.

Pillow Police

In 1999, we went on vacation to Hawaii. My nephew, Justin, was 18 at the time. He came along with us to help me with Michael and Jamie who were 8 and 5. We had originally planned to stay for five days. On Day Four, we decided to extend the trip for three more days. We stayed at the Hyatt for the first part of the trip and transferred to the Marriott for the second part.

In 1998, a new toy called a Furby had come out, an owl-looking, furry electronic robot. It was a must-have for the 1998 holiday season, so, of course, Santa brought one for both Michael and Jamie. The Furbies came to Hawaii with us. Furbies would talk "Furbish" until they learned English from their owner. They made weird noises all of the time.

The day we moved to the Marriott, Michael and Jamie opened their suitcases, and each Furby was snuggled inside a pillow.

I don't remember if it was me or Justin who asked, "Where did you get the pillows?"

Staring at the floor, they both sheepishly said, "The Hyatt."

"Don't you know there are pillow police?" Justin demanded.

Both kids had big eyes and that *uh-oh* look. For the next couple of days, we milked it. They did everything we asked them to do, no whining or protesting.

On the Fourth of July, we were on the beach on a blanket next to the boardwalk. I saw a golf cart coming our way and said, "The pillow police!"

Instantly, Michael dove under the blanket.

That was enough. When he reappeared, I told them there weren't any pillow police. We were just teasing. The relief was palpable.

When we left Hawaii, we returned the pillows to the Hyatt.

I thought of the episode as "Roughing Up the Cubs." Not only was it a good lesson in staying honest, but it also was a lesson for, "If you dish it out, you gotta be able to take it." It's a matter of survival in our family.

As you can imagine, that story has become a family classic. Michael and Jamie can hang with the best of us.

In 2015, Jamie's team earned a silver medal at the Mozart Cup in Salzburg and went on to the World Championships in Canada to place 8th overall. At the world championships, Japan placed 14th overall.

In 1922, J.C. and Lotta had the world at their fingertips...skating to the "The World is Ours," Jamie's team: "Run like you're born to fly, live like you'll never die, the world is ours."

To watch the USA, go to YouTube:
Mozart Cup 2015 - Miami University - Short Program
https://www.youtube.com/watch?v=W1hgzZPY8nc
Music: The World is Ours by David Correy and Aloe Blacc

To watch Team Japan, go to YouTube:
2015 World Synchro Champs SP Team Japan
https://www.youtube.com/watch?v=fadlSi_4NRI&t=203s
Music: The Rose by Bette Midler

A LUCY MOMENT
CFOs and Barking Dogs

To be honest, I'm not sure that J.C. and Lotta—or J.C.'s mother Mary Churchill—would know what to do with me, with all of my escapades and irreverent humor. I say, join the club. My Homeowners Association, my clients, the gas attendants holding AK-47's, McKenna, the cabbie…who does? I am definitely not the norm, but as my dad would say, I wouldn't have it any other way.

In 1992, when I transferred to the Consulting Division of Corroon & Black, their offices were in San Diego, an hour and a half from my house. As a result, I negotiated working from home four days a week.

In those days, people were just starting to work from home. The practice was generally frowned upon, so phone calls became more stressful. The other person should never know you were at home. Unfortunately, I had a yappy dachshund named Spike.

I would carefully put Spike in a far bedroom whenever I had an important call. That worked out well, until one day when I answered an unexpected call from Matthew Mazdyasni, Chief Financial Officer for California Primary Physicians (CPP) in downtown Los Angeles, one of my largest clients.

As soon as I answered, I remembered that Spike was on the loose in the house.

Sure enough, I heard his toenails clicking on the stairs. I could almost hear Jaws music in the background. Spike came around the corner, and I gave him a wide-eyed look, followed by the hairy, evil eye.

Instantly, that eight pounds of terror went into a full-out barking session. The jig was up.

I immediately said, "We hire real dogs around here!"

Matthew started laughing, and we continued our conversation. Problem solved. Humor is a good lubricant when things aren't going your way.

Today, I have a fourteen-pound Cavalier. She's like a child. As soon as I get on a call, she barks for me to throw her stuffed alligator. Now, I spend my time throwing her alligator while I am talking.

Moral of the story: if you work at home, you might be better off with a cat.

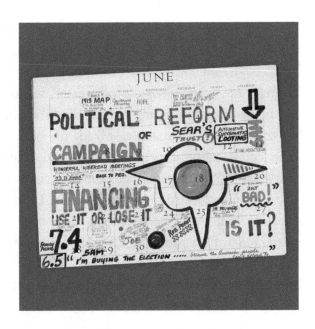

CHAPTER 11

Chaos is Opportunity

A pessimist sees difficulty in every opportunity, the optimist sees opportunity in every difficulty.[61]
~Winston Churchill

Closers are hard to find. They design the deals and get signatures on contracts. Closers comprise about 5 percent of the population. Because they are in high demand, they make a lot of money.

---

[61] https://www.brainyquote.com/quotes/winston_churchill_103739

Most people find it hard to ask for the order, but I was always excited to play for a win. To me, business was one big game made up of strategy, winners and losers.

Our company called closers producers. A technical producer knew the details about a product, pitched the points that best applied to a specific prospect, asked for the order and got the deal done. Technical producers were also hard to find.

A visionary technical producer examines chaos for ways to create new opportunity. When the Chicken Littles of this world run away crying, "The sky is falling," visionary technical producers dash toward the problem. They stare at it from different angles until they figure out how to fix it.

"They stare at it from different angles until they figure out how to fix it."

Growing up with my artist father, I learned to look at every picture from different perspectives.

Dad painted every Sunday while listening to his favorite music. When I was little, I would skip around the circle in our house to the likes of "Hello Dolly." When I was older, he played music like Gershwin's "Rhapsody in Blue." My dad would rock to the music as he painted that week's abstract masterpiece, and I would rock along with him.

When he was ready, he would hang the painting on the wooden fence alongside our driveway where it stayed for several days. Each day, he would tilt it to a new angle and stare at it. He would add touches from that angle. He said abstract paintings should look great regardless of how the canvas turned.

In my career, I learned to tilt any circumstance and look at it from all angles until I found an opportunity no one else saw.

In the 1990s, I was at lunch with the CEO of Bristol Park Medical Group, Pat Kapsner. He was familiar with my dad's art. Over a Caesar salad, I said, "Isn't it odd that I didn't get my dad's artistic talent?"

He said, "Therese, your art is your vision in business."

I think that's why I loved my deals so much, and why I loved the game.

Where there is chaos, there is opportunity.

My partners, Jerry Sullivan and Frank McKenna, were visionary technical producers. They were innovators in the industry.

1. Sullivan created the first structured settlement contract with Lloyd's of London.

   Chaos: Up until the 1980s, insurance companies made large payouts as lump sums. Too many of these in a short span of time, and the company could feel some stress. Often the client also felt stress when that individual wasn't accustomed to managing large sums of money.

   Opportunity: Make these payouts in regular increments, rather than all at once. The client could depend on payments over time, and the insurance company didn't feel as much of a pinch. This was a win-win.

2. McKenna created the first capitation stop-loss contract with Lloyd's of London.

   Chaos: In the 1990s, the risk shifted from the HMOs to the doctors as the providers of care. Physicians received a flat rate per member. These physicians had to manage that per-member-per-month (PMPM) rate and try to make money. If a patient became sick with a catastrophic illness, and the physician and hospital bills amounted to $75,000, the physician's group was on the hook. Many of them stayed in the red.

Opportunity: Shifting the risk to Lloyd's of London relieved the doctors of this dilemma of wanting to care for their patients but knowing that too much expense could provide too much risk. This coverage provided "sleep insurance" for the doctors who could now sleep at night, and a whole new line of coverage for McKenna to sell. Another win-win.

3. I created the first retention-only contract for healthcare providers.

Chaos: Physician groups paid insurance premiums for their employees and also provided the care for their employees. In the case of Friendly Hills, 90 percent of their employees signed up for their own doctors' care. Essentially, their money made a circle and came back to them. I thought of a way the Medical Groups could keep those premiums and thus lower their costs.

Opportunity: The Medical Group would spread the risk across 500,000 members vs. the regular stop-loss on 1,500 employees, while also paying out less. This would cost substantially less than traditional self-insured stop-loss. In addition, this cut their administration costs in half, and their cash flow increased. The medical groups would save money simply by making a few adjustments to their HMO policy, and I had an emerging product to take to other prospective medical groups. This was a win-win-win.

If you are an employer, and you have a visionary technical producer in your company, throw lots of money at them. Give them equity (ownership) and keep them on board. They are the entrepreneurial type who can make you a lot of money. On the other hand, they might have an epiphany and leave you to start their own business.

A Surprising Win-Win

Being a visionary technical producer had its benefits in my personal life, sometimes in unexpected ways. When I went through a divorce in 2011, I put the Coral Cay house up for sale after living there for thirteen years. When shopping for a new place, I saw my current home listed for sale: 2400 square feet, 3 bedrooms and a three-car garage. I could convert one of the garages into a room for Michael. This condo was an end unit, so it had the largest patio of the models. Pacific Coast Highway was a cross street, so it was steps away from the beach.

On paper, it was perfect.

When I stepped inside the condo, I had one of those wow moments. The window treatments were ceiling to floor, and the ceilings were raised. On the left was a fireplace with a gigantic mirror over it, giving the illusion of a room double its size. The railings and stairways were made of wood and custom wrought iron.

The owner was a designer, and her family was in the construction industry. The workmanship was top notch.

The dining room had a big medieval-looking table with large oversized chairs wrapped in fabric. Like I said, I was sold on my first step through the door.

You can imagine my disappointment when my realtor called me that night and said, "The owner doesn't want to sell. She's close to bankruptcy, and she's overwhelmed."

The owner had chaos. I immediately started turning her problem around in my mind to find the opportunity. Keep your eye on the prize and figure out how to get it. Aim high and refuse the no.

"Aim high and refuse the no."

I saw three problems converging on this gorgeous condo. The owner was running out of money. The bank was about to foreclose on a property that would move from their asset column to the liability column. Then my problem: I needed a place to live.

A few hours later, I had a solution. I called the realtor to set up a meeting with the owner. I offered her cash as a short sale and suggested we go to the bank together with an all-cash offer. I also offered to buy the furniture outside of escrow, so she would end up with some personal cash. She was all smiles.

It worked. The bank approved our first offer (which, of course, makes me feel like I should have offered less). The owner walked away with dignity after all of the work she had put into the condo. She sent me a note later, saying I was an angel for helping her out.

My condo with my dad's painting on the back wall.

I acquired that beautiful, perfect condo. Everyone was happy, and we had a win-win-win. To top it off, the Coral Cay escrow and the new condo closed within 24 hours of each other, which never happens. This time, one could say the chaos created magic.

Where there is chaos, there is opportunity.

After everything was said and done, my realtor, Sandy Powers, who sells in Huntington Beach and Newport Beach said, "If you ever write a book, I am going to have my team read it!" This stuff works.

Here are the principles from that deal.

- I Can - I didn't give up. I refused the no.
- Pay your dues. Don't be entitled – For years, I had learned the art of making deals.
- Luck is where preparation meets opportunity – I was prepared to come up with a winning strategy. As a matter of fact, I loved it.
- Where there is chaos, there is opportunity – I came up with a solution to get the deal done
- Don't leave money on the table – Oh, I definitely left money on the table. Without blinking, the bank accepted my offer which was $115,000 below asking price. I could have gone lower. As I have said, "Pigs get fat. Hogs get slaughtered," so I left it at that.

Difficulties mastered are opportunities won.[62]
~Winston Churchill

---

[62] https://www.goodreads.com/quotes/27621-difficulties-mastered-are-opportunities-won

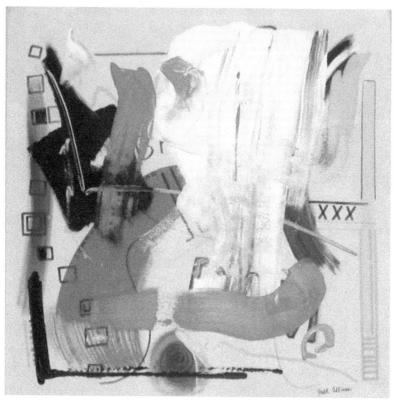

1999-2003 NEW CENTURY

"Water was the new gold."

THE ALLISON HERITAGE:

California's Little Civil War

In the mid-1800s to early 1900s, California was a land of unlimited opportunities. When the Gold Rush was over, those thousands of people who had poured into the California Territory soon built homes and settled down. Newcomers continued to arrive, especially after the transcontinental railroad was complete. All those families needed water. To put it simply, water became the new gold.

My great-great-grandfather, Robert Allison, and later my grandfather, J.C. Allison, were immersed in it. This was the quintessential example of where there is chaos, there is opportunity.

Where there is chaos, there is opportunity.

This situation brought about the deal of the century that became the backdrop for the movie *Chinatown* (as in, "Forget it, Jake. It's Chinatown.") starring Jack Nicholson and Faye Dunaway.

Chinatown was loosely based on the book *The California Water Wars*[63] which told about a series of disputes over Southern California water at the beginning of the 20th century. *Chinatown* won Best Original Screenplay and was nominated for numerous Oscars and Golden Globes. Today, it is considered one of the classic movies of all time.

History shows that William Mulholland, superintendent of the local Water Company and his long-time friend, Frederick

---

[63] https://en.wikipedia.org/wiki/California_water_wars

Eaton, the mayor of Los Angeles, came up with a scheme to divert water from the rich farmlands and orchards of Owens Valley and bring it to the San Fernando Valley north of Los Angeles.

Mulholland told the Los Angeles public they were running out of water, making the problem seem far greater than it was. Mulholland also misled residents of the Owens Valley by saying the new aqueduct would only use overflows in the Owens Valley, while he actually planned on turning that farmland into a desert by taking all their water.

In 1907, Eaton traveled to Washington D.C. to meet with advisers of Theodore Roosevelt. He convinced them that Los Angeles needed the water more than the Owens Valley farmlands.[64] He failed to tell them that the water would end up in the yet-undeveloped San Fernando Valley, not the city of Los Angeles.

The Los Angeles Suburban Homes Company was made up of Harrison Gray Otis (Publisher of the *L.A. Times*), his son-in-law Harry Chandler, General Moses H. Sherman, Hobart Whitley, Henry Huntington (Huntington Beach), Isaac Newton Van Nuys, James Boon Lankershim and Eli Clark, among others. This syndicate purchased 47,500 acres, nearly the entire south half of the San Fernando Valley for $2,500,000, or just under $53 an acre.[65]

They all made a fortune.

This venture became a Monopoly game involving water, transportation, real estate and the press. Who better to sell the idea to the people of Los Angeles than Harrison Gray Otis, the publisher and owner of the *Los Angeles Times*? In those days, word of mouth, public speeches and the newspaper were the main methods of communication, so the *Los Angeles Times* had a

---

[64] Ibid.

[65] https://en.wikipedia.org/wiki/Moses_Sherman#San_Fernando_Valley

huge advantage in persuading the public to vote in favor of the bonds needed for building the aqueduct and lining the pockets of its owners in the process.

In a desperate attempt to protect their dying farmland, Owens Valley farmers resorted to dynamite sabotage of pipelines and aqueducts to return the water to its original course. It was an epic struggle between the haves and have nots.

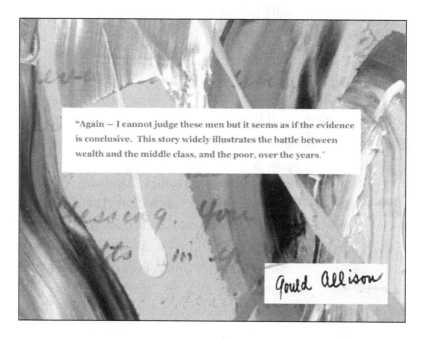

"Again — I cannot judge these men but it seems as if the evidence is conclusive. This story widely illustrates the battle between wealth and the middle class, and the poor, over the years."

Gould Allison

Because of shenanigans like this, my dad had a lifelong disdain of big business and big wealth. Interesting that he used his inheritance of $6,000 as a down payment to purchase my childhood home in La Canada, which was full of the uber wealthy. Dad became an activist in the area, a vocal and visible thorn in the side of developers for decades.

I believe his dislike of big wealth had a lot to do with his overworked father, J.C. Allison, dying of a heart attack when Dad was six. The only thing Dad remembered about his father was his governess taking him into his father's office in their La Jolla house. Big business had taken his father away, even before J.C. died.

At the time of the *Chinatown* story, J.C. was only 25 years old, working on the Colorado River below the border in Mexico. He was not involved in the chicanery. However, over the following years he formed relationships with many of the players in that drama and became one of their dependable and respected engineers.

Uber-wealthy businessmen loved my grandfather's vision and engineering prowess when it came to building infrastructure. When J.C. Allison had an idea, these men saw dollar signs, BIG dollar signs. It was easy for a syndicate of investors to hire J.C. with his wide experience around the Colorado River, his ability to come up with a viable strategy that would take a project to completion, his ability to negotiate deals, and his knack for turning a problem into profit.

Harry Chandler and Moses H. Sherman were the primary investors in a syndicate known as the Colorado River Land Company (CRLC). They hired my grandfather as an engineer for their various real estate interests in the Imperial Valley of lower California and Mexico.

Worth $7 billion in today's dollars, Harry Chandler once had the largest real estate empire in the United States and was probably the most influential human being in the Southwest. Moses H. Sherman was a land developer and railway magnate. In 1906, he was worth the equivalent of $150 million in today's dollars. United in the CLRC, Chandler and Sherman carried a lot of influence.

The Colorado River Land Company hired my grandfather to manage 860,000 acres south of the border, primarily cotton, that Harry Chandler had purchased in 1900. In square miles, that property was the size of almost the entire West Coast. Besides this, J.C. also had other projects and interests. No wonder he hardly knew his young son.

When is enough, enough?

The Allison's in Hollywood

Hollywood is the place where making things happen is an art form. It is also a place where my grandparents rubbed elbows with the movie industry... I was born there.

As the lore goes, after the Laguna Theatre opened in 1922, on movie premier nights, J.C. and Lotta would take separate cars and race from La Jolla up Pacific Coast Highway to the theater. They always attended because of my grandfather's association with Harry Chandler and General Moses H. Sherman who founded Hollywood.

I can imagine them in their glamorous attire arriving in front of the theater as VIPs, walking arm in arm down the red carpet, jewels glittering, with the spotlight on them (ok, a little poetic license here!) The first red carpet was rolled out in 1922 at the first Hollywood Premiere—*Robin Hood* starring Douglas Fairbanks at the Egyptian Grauman Theatre. From that point on, the red carpet and Hollywood became synonymous.

Five men, including General Sherman and Harry Chandler, formed a syndicate to build the first hillside planned community in Los Angeles. One of the men, Hobart Whitley, brought Paramount, Warner Bros., RKO, and Columbia to the city. Whitley is considered the "Father of Hollywood."

The films and stars of Hollywood helped make the state the center of worldwide attention. The American dream became the California dream. The Hollywood sign became a universal sign for beckoning people to come for glamour, fame and fortune.

Harry Chandler constructed the original Hollywood sign, but it started out as Hollywoodland. His original intent was to bring attention (in a very bold way!) to the homes for sale in the Hollywoodland development. At night, the sign would flash lights on "Holly" then "wood" then "land"—Vegas style in 1923 Los Angeles.[66]

At the height of Hollywood's Golden Age in the 1930s, the movie industry was one of the largest businesses in the United States, even in the depths of the Depression. When I was growing up, Dad mentioned his parents' connection, but I didn't understand what that meant until much later.

My dad had his own connection to Hollywood. My mom passed away in 1998. A few years later, Dad reconnected with an old friend from high school, named Helen Peppard-Davies. She was an actress and grew up around the theater as her father owned the Old Globe Theatre in San Diego. The venue was inspired by Shakespeare's outdoor theatres.

Helen's ex-husband was actor George Peppard, most famous for his role in *Breakfast at Tiffany's* with co-star Audrey Hepburn. My dad's calendar reminded me that he and I went to Christmas dinner at her house and met her children. We had a great time. I guess you could say that we had "Dinner at Peppard's!"

A lot of Hollywood executives lived in La Canada. No wonder my high school class of 1979 had a Hollywood theme for the yearbook. Cara and I both worked on the yearbook our senior year. We had a group of very talented people on the yearbook team. Many of the pages had scenes from various movies with our classmates positioned in them.

Our senior prom had a Hollywood theme as well, called "It Happened One Night," a romantic comedy set to entertain

[66] "Hollywood," History.com, August 21, 2018.

people during the Depression. Movies gave people a weekly escape from their daily struggles.

As I was dancing at the prom in the ballroom of The Ambassador Hotel in downtown L.A., I could imagine my grandparents arriving at the "It Happened One Night" premiere in 1934, dripping with furs and jewels. Oh, I forgot to mention, I was the tomboy who became Prom Queen that year.

"I was the tomboy who became Prom Queen that year."

My grandfather connected to the founders of Hollywood...my grandparents attending the first premieres... Hollywood executives who lived in La Canada...my dad's connection to the Peppard's...Prom Queen when the theme was a movie from my grandparents' time...Hollywood is my birthplace—you might think it's all coincidence. I think it is synchronicity.

1978 me in Juniors vs. Seniors rivalry game. We beat the Seniors

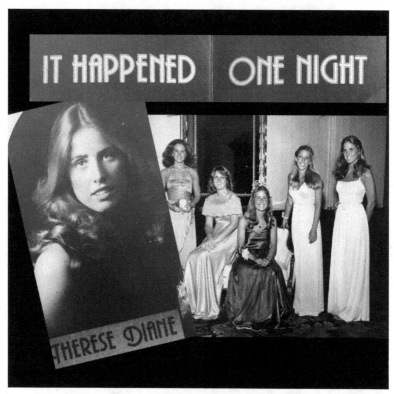

Prom court from left: Holly Hagen, Linda Boss, me,
Cara Badger and Karen Hench

"I was the tomboy who became
Prom Queen."

MENTORING MICHAEL: You Can Play

Chaos and opportunity are not always about money. These are the values we should teach our kids. Sometimes the chaos can be social injustice, and the opportunity to stand for someone else.

Like a good abstract painting can be tilted in any direction, and still look great, people can live their lives from different angles as well. We are all different, but we are all the same.

In 2012, a movement sprang up called You Can Play, a social activism campaign dedicated to the eradication of homophobia in sports. The slogan said, "If you can play, you can play." Michael had a friend and fellow hockey player who was gay. To show their support for their teammate, the team participated in the You Can Play campaign and put together a video on behalf of UCLA Hockey. The script went like this:

What matters - If you can shoot, you can shoot.

If you can pass, you can pass.

If you can block, you can block.

You know what doesn't matter to me, is if you are gay or straight.

If you can play, you can play.

In the chaos of injustice comes the opportunity to show compassion and acceptance. These opportunities are priceless

To view this Go to YouTube:

You Can Play - UCLA Bruins Hockey and Figure Skating.mov
https://www.youtube.com/watch?v=go_8LihYHwA

A LUCY MOMENT
The Tea Party

I always figured that my airhead moments happened because my mind was preoccupied with business. However, after I retired, I soon realized that my Lucy Moments continued, and I had no one else to blame.

Many people over the years have said that I have angels who help me, as everything always works out. For this trip, I can imagine the angels on the bullhorn in heaven, "We need reinforcements. She's driving in Boston… We don't get paid enough!"

Jamie's Colonial Classic competition in Worcester, Massachusetts, ended late. My flight the next morning was at 7:30 a.m. out of Logan International Airport. I had to get up at O'Dark…4:30 a.m. East Coast time. Logan was 55 minutes from the hotel, so I felt comfortable and didn't rush.

After all, I'd given myself plenty of time, and I had a Garmin Navigation System in the car. I was locked, loaded and Lucy-proof.

After driving for about forty-five minutes, my instinct kept telling me something wasn't right. Nothing around me said, *Airport*—no wide highway, no signs, no traffic. But I had Garmin and "she" was telling me otherwise. I drove for a while longer. She told me to get off and go through a small town.

At this point, I became concerned. Where was the wide highway? I continue to listen to her, and we start going down side streets. *OK, that's enough.* I stopped driving so I could look at her illuminated map. It was still dark. Her map showed a symbol of my car on a dotted line that meant off road. *What?*

She insisted that I turn right. The moment I rounded the corner, I saw planes taking off on the other side of a large body of water. A moment later, I realized I was looking at the Boston Harbor—you know, the place where they dumped all the tea!

Garmin and I were not havin' a party. Her "mis-guidance" was gonna cost me. She definitely had some *splainin'* to do. I turned around and muddled my way to the airport.

I missed my flight. Four hours and $600 later, I was in the air on my way home.

I can see the headline now, "Garmin Dumps Driver into Boston Harbor."

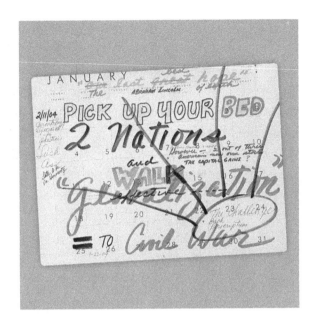

CHAPTER 12

Be a Cheerleader

To win in the marketplace, you must first win in the workplace.[67] ~Doug Conant

A few years ago, a friend of a friend (I'll call him Jim) went to interview for a job. The waiting room was in disarray with a lot of chairs pushed to one side. Shortly after Jim sat down, a man came out of the inner office. He started stacking the chairs and moving them out of the room. After about fifteen

[67] https://www.yourthoughtpartner.com/blog/10-inspiring-quotes-from-successful-ceos-to-help-you-win-at-employee-engagement

minutes of hard work, he pushed the last stack of chairs into the next room.

The man returned to the waiting room and told Jim the interview was over. Surprised, Jim asked why. The man replied, "You failed the test." Again, Jim asked why. The man introduced himself as the CEO of the company and pointed out that Jim sat by while someone else worked and had never offered to help.

Don't stop your interview before it starts. Treat people the way you want to be treated.

Treat others the way you want to be treated.

At McKenna & Associates, this was our approach when working with other companies. We wanted our clients and joint venture partners to feel like Rockstars.

Gloria Mayer from Friendly Hills was a prime example. The first time I met Gloria, she told me I should be fired. I continued to treat her with kindness and respect. When I came up with the retention concept, I gave Gloria all of the credit. In a major turnaround, Gloria championed me from that point on.

After I joined McKenna & Associates, we took Gloria to London. Talk about treating her like royalty. She had entree into Lloyd's of London to meet with the best underwriters in the world. She enjoyed fine dining and 5-star accommodations. She went on private tours with Jerry's driver in and around London. Sure, this was a working trip where she had to present her intellectual knowledge of the managed care industry and where it was going, but the perks were incredible.

Besides Dr. Barnett, Gloria was the one who put me on her Board of Directors for their non-profit organization providing free healthcare for underprivileged children. My relationship with Gloria opened doors for me. I had the opportunity to expand my experience base by volunteering as a board member in a much-needed area.

In business, you have to take your ego out of it. This is about building business. It's not about you.

"Take your ego out of it."

A company culture that embraces this approach will inspire their employees, treat them with respect...and empower them to achieve their goals. Treat your team members like you would a client or a significant revenue source. The more you care about them, the more they will care about you and your clients.

"Treat your team members like you would a client."

Always aim to make your clients look good to their higher ups. You will be amazed at the loyalty they provide in return. If they change employers, most likely you will obtain their business at their new employer. This is how I had accounts follow me when someone changed companies.

"Make your clients look good to their higher ups."

Treat vendors, underwriters and representatives the way you would want to be treated. Gift baskets, thank you notes, a fun lunch filled with Lucy stories—you would be surprised at how much easier it will be to work with them and get favorable pricing and terms if you are thoughtful, kind and friendly. Just be a good person. It's becoming a lost art.

"Just be a good person."

Always make your bosses look good. Give them credit for stuff you put together for them. Bad mouthing your boss or going around your boss for your own gain are two major mistakes. If you are a great employee, you will be noticed.

"Always make your bosses look good."

People who are groomed to climb the ladder in a good company have shown good character traits in their current position. You don't move up by putting others down. If you make this mistake, no one from the higher ups will want you working for them.

If you are moving up the ladder, be aware of higher ups you don't report to and get acquainted with their agendas. Practice looking at the bigger picture. Learn what people want and how to give it to them. For example, some want speed for quick delivery. Others want accuracy so there's no backtracking. Find out what others value, and you'll have a sure way to create a win for both of you.

"Be aware of higher ups and get acquainted with their agendas."

Last, bide your time. Your opportunity will come whether with your current company or another one.

My dad.

My dad at San Diego High School circa 1948

"In life and in business,
be a cheerleader."

THE ALLISON HERITAGE:

Lincoln—Illinois' Favored Son

In 1850, Robert Whitney Waterman traveled over the plains for the Gold Rush. In 1851, he returned to his family in Wilmington, Illinois. In 1854, he helped form the Illinois Republican Party. In 1856, he was one of two Illinois delegates to attend the first Republican National Convention. The other delegate was his friend Abraham Lincoln.

In 1860, Robert Whitney Waterman played a major role in Abraham Lincoln's winning the White House. As a delegate from Illinois, Waterman was in Lincoln's backyard and knew the key players. He helped deliver Illinois for Lincoln which helped Lincoln reach the White House. It was never about Waterman per se. It was about Lincoln and what he represented in supporting abolition and ultimately the Thirteenth Amendment.

Waterman was a cheerleader.

In 1873, Waterman returned to California. He became partners with my great-great-grandfather, Robert Allison, and they purchased Cuyamaca together in 1886. In 1887, Waterman became the 17th Governor of California.[68] As governor, his nickname was "Old Honesty" because he kicked anyone out of his office who tried to bribe him.[69]

Robert Allison married the governor's relative, Tempa Waterman, my great-great-grandmother.

The election of Abraham Lincoln in November 1860 was perhaps the most significant election in American history. It brought Lincoln to power at a time of great national crisis, as the country was coming apart over the issue of slavery.

---

[68] https://en.wikipedia.org/wiki/Robert_Waterman_(governor)
[69] Ibid.

The 1860 Republican nomination was a game of strategy, and Abraham Lincoln definitely played for keeps. He pulled out all of the stops and outfoxed his opponent, William Seward of New York, although Seward was clearly the frontrunner.

LEFT: Robert Waterman   CENTER: 1860 Republican Convention
RIGHT: Abraham Lincoln

In 1860, Chicago had a population of 100,000, and Lincoln was the "favored son" of Illinois. Since the Republican convention was in Chicago that year, many people attending the convention wanted to help get Lincoln elected.

Here are some of the strategies of the Lincoln campaign:

— They brought in two men with extraordinarily loud voices to lead the cheering.

— They printed counterfeit tickets, so Lincoln supporters could show up early and take the seats of Seward supporters.

— Right before Lincoln was announced as the victor, the crowd became silent... followed by an eruption from the audience that was so deafening, the only way people could tell the cannons were firing was by watching the smoke drift from the barrels.

— Strategy was everything.

President Lincoln saved the country despite a brutal Civil War that almost tore it apart. Most scholars say he was the best President of all time. I can definitely see why. Abraham Lincoln practiced the same principles I followed in order to become successful in my eighteen years of business. They are universal, and they will take you to success, too. Here are seven of them:

(1) Lincoln left his office to circulate amongst the troops.

Early on in the Civil War, Lincoln made it a point to meet every single Union soldier. In 1861, he spent more time on the road than he did in Washington. Business guru Tom Peters called this approach "Managing by Wandering Around."[70]

- People do business with people they like.
- Always dance with the partner who brought you to the dance.
- Treat others the way you want to be treated.

(2) Lincoln was constantly alert for dependable information, so he could make the best decisions.

Lincoln practically lived at the telegraph office of the War Department, so he would be instantly available when news came in. The telephone had not been invented yet, and a foot messenger took too long. Instead of waiting in his office, he personally went to the source.

---

[70] "'Management by Wandering Around,' according to Tom Peters," ReliablePlant.com https://www.reliableplant.com/view/26392/managing-by-wandering-around

- Luck is where preparation meets opportunity.
- Where there is chaos, there is opportunity.

(3) He studied and practiced leadership and strategy until it became second nature.

Lincoln served in the Illinois militia in 1832. He served in the Illinois House of Representatives in 1834 and in the US House of Representatives in 1846. After one term in Congress, he returned to his home state and opened a law practice where he worked in the trenches for the next fourteen years. In 1860, he was elected President of the United States and took office in 1861.

- Pay your dues. Don't be entitled.
- I can.

(4) Lincoln used persuasion rather than coercion.
In his Temperance Address, Lincoln said,

> If you would win a man to your cause, first convince him that you are his sincere friend. Therein is a drop of honey that catches his heart, which, say what he will, is the great high road to his reason, and which, when once gained, you will find by little trouble in convincing his judgement of the justice of your cause, if indeed that cause really be a just one.[71]

He also said, "Do I not destroy my enemies when I make them my friends?"[72]

- Be true to you.
- People do business with people they like.
- Treat others the way you want to be treated.

---

[71] http://www.abrahamlincolnonline.org/lincoln/speeches/temperance.htm
[72] https://www.goodreads.com/quotes/10667-do-i-not-destroy-my-enemies-when-i-make-them

(5) Lincoln led others by following their lead.

He gave those under him the correct perception that they were the ones leading the way. Lincoln gave credit where credit was due and took responsibility when things went wrong. He made his employees look good.[73]

> *"Fail to honor people, they fail to honor you. But of a good leader, who talks little, when his work is done, his aim fulfilled, they will all say 'We did this ourselves.'"*[74] ~Lao Tsu

- Own up to your mistakes. Come up with a solution.
- When you don't know the answer, say so.
- Always take the high road.

(6) Lincoln encouraged innovation.

Abraham Lincoln is the only United States President who held a patent for his own invention. He found a way to make grounded boats more buoyant.[75]

As President, he regularly called on his staff to hear their ideas, look at new advances and learn from them. He fostered a culture of entrepreneurship that encouraged innovation.[76] He knew the value of visionary technical producers, and he filled his team with them.

[73] Eric Barker, "Lessons from Lincoln: 5 Leadership Tips History and Science Agree On."

[74] Lao Tzu (Author), Hua-Ching Ni (Translator), *The Complete Works of Lao Tzu: Tao Teh Ching and Hua Hu Ching* (Kaipamangalam, India: SevenStar Communications, August 8, 2013).

[75] Donald T. Phillips, *Lincoln On Leadership: Executive Strategies for Tough Times* (Published by Amazon Services for Donald T Phillips & Associates, November 17, 2013).

[76] Ibid.

- I Can.
- Luck is where preparation meets opportunity.

(7) He influenced people through storytelling.

Lincoln learned how to get his point across or diffuse a tense situation by telling humorous stories. He said, "I have learned from long experience that plain people...are more easily influenced through the medium of a broad and humorous illustration than in any other way."[77]

"When he gently led people to laugh with him, his opponents lost their advantage."

When he gently led people to laugh with him, his opponents lost their advantage. Research from Stanford backs this idea up.[78] I couldn't agree more. When you tell a story, the listener has a chance to get to know you at another level, and that can win them over.

Paraphrased from *Lincoln's Yarns and Stories*, by Alexander K. McClure is the following story from Lincoln's days as President.

One day at a Cabinet meeting, the discussion turned to growing tensions with England and France that could possibly escalate into war. Two Cabinet members wanted to take an aggressive stance against these countries.

Lincoln asked, "Why take more risk than are absolutely necessary?"

"We must maintain our honor," one of them said.

"The world will think we are cowards," the other one added.

---

[77] https://time.com/37025/lessons-from-lincoln-5-leadership-tips-history-and-science-agree-on/

[78] Stanford Storytelling Project, https://storytelling.stanford.edu/

Lincoln remained calm. His tone was reasonable. "But why run a greater risk when we can take a smaller one? The less risk, the better." He turned to the group. "That reminds me of a story about a hero on the front lines during a recent battle. Bullets were flying thick and fast all around him.

"He finally had all he could take. He threw down his gun and ran.

"As he was dashing along at top speed, dodging people and bullets. He ran into an officer who pointed his weapon and shouted, 'Go back to your regiment at once, or I will shoot you!'

"'Shoot!' the soldier exclaimed before he raced away. 'What's one bullet after all I've been through?'"[79]

When Lincoln got a chuckle, he knew he was on the right track. The Number One negotiation tactic Harvard Business teaches its MBA students: They need to like you.[80]

Honestly, this works!

[79] Alexander K. McClure, *Lincoln's Yarns and Stories*, (Project Gutenberg: Release Date: February, 2001 [EBook #2517] Last Updated: November 15, 2016) https://www.gutenberg.org/files/2517/2517-h/2517-h.htm#link2H_4_0018
[80] https://www.bakadesuyo.com/2013/08/negotiation-process/

Mentoring Jamie

My grandfather was conservative, and my father was liberal. I am a combination of both. I definitely picked up compassion for others from my dad (and he from Lotta). My kids have picked it up from me.

To our family, sports is a microcosm for life. So many life lessons happen in sports.

Whenever I went to Jamie's skating competitions, I would see Jamie cheering for her teammates as she moved to the more difficult teams. She never forgot where she started. By the time that she made it to the senior team, she and her friends were cheerleaders for each other.

In life, no matter what team you're on, genuine connections with other people and sincere happiness for each other's success—that's what counts.

In life and in business, be a cheerleader!

'A' LUCY MOMENT
Me and Sheryl Crow

In March 2002, Sheryl Crow's album, C'mon c'mon debuted. Her song "Soak up the Sun" was #1 on the billboard charts for one month. Crow's co-writer, Jeff Trott, came up with the idea for the song on a flight from Portland, Oregon, to New York. Portland was soaking in rain and he was headed to New York to soak up some sun. On the five-hour flight, he came up with the song in his head. I completely get this. Some of my best writing has happened on planes.

In 2002, three partners in our company were at an AON meeting at their headquarters in Chicago. Thankfully, it was summer. Several of our producing employees came along, all men. As usual, it was me and the boys.

After our meeting, we all headed for lunch. We got off of the elevator and walked toward the restaurant.

That's when things got weird. First, I noticed the security guards whispering and looking at me. Uh oh. My Lucy radar started pinging. I had déjà vu, except this wasn't First Class.

I looked down. My shoes matched, so it wasn't that. My stomach tensed. Maybe my skirt was ripped.

I asked a smiling security guard where the restroom was. Inside I completed surveillance of my suit and skirt for wardrobe failure…all good. I was even having a good hair day, and nothing in my teeth.

What in the heck? I couldn't figure out for the life of me why they were whispering and staring.

Trying to look natural, I found the guys' table and sat down. A few minutes later, the waiters started talking to each other and staring at me.

The hair on my arms stood up. I pictured news flashes on the television from America's Most Wanted.

All smiles, our waiter finally came over and told us that the hotel staff thought I was Sheryl Crow. She had a concert in Chicago that night for her "Soak up the Sun" Tour.

I burst out laughing and said, "If I were really Sheryl Crow, do you think I'd be hanging around with these insurance schmoes?"

At that time, my hair was much lighter, so I can see their confusion. I had been told that I looked like her many times before. Of course, the guys called me "Sheryl" for the rest of the trip. Hey, I'll take it.

Sheryl Crow and me

To listen to Sheryl sing Steve McQueen when she was on her "Soak Up The Sun" tour in 2002 go to YouTube: **Sheryl Crow - "Steve McQueen" live 2002 stereo**
https://www.youtube.com/watch?v=he7e7NiWeoA

CHAPTER 13

Build a Golden Circle of Friends

Be true to your work, your word, and your friend.[81]
~Henry David Thoreau

On a crisp morning in 1965, I was sitting on the curb on Commonwealth Avenue with three other kids, waiting for the bus. We were neighbors on our first day of kindergarten. I wiggled my shoes, admiring those gleaming black leather Mary Jane's. I looked at the shoes on the girl next to me, white patent-leather Mary Jane's. We both had blankies. Hers was white, and

---

[81] http://www.quotationspage.com/quote/34411.html

mine was pink. I looked at her shyly and lisped, "Hi, I'm Therese." She said, "Hi, I'm Cara."

That was fifty-five years ago. We still talk two times a week.

Her dad was conservative, and mine was liberal. Maybe we were switched at birth!

So many images flash through my mind when I think of Cara—sleepovers, swimming pools and playdates, trick or treating, listening to Jethro Tull's *Aqualung* until our parents went crazy... running up Commonwealth to her house after my parents told me my sister had died.

We were on the prom court together. We were on the yearbook staff our senior year together. We made TA burgers on English muffins too many times to remember.

Once I was thrown into the pool with her dad's six-foot boa constrictor named Kaa. The snake frequently got lost in the house, and one time they found him in the dashboard of Cara's car. I was always on edge at their house, peeking into corners and under the chair before I sat down. I'll be the first to admit that my family was a bit unusual, but Cara's family...kept things exciting.

Cara and I were college roommates, singing Tina Turner's "Proud Mary" and "The Hill Are Alive" from *The Sound of Music* at the top of our lungs in the worst soprano you have ever heard, laughing till we cried. Our children arrived a month apart with all of the milestones that life has to offer. Through a lifetime of friendship, the one tenant that has held us together: we always have each other's backs.

The same is true of Kathy Rhoads.

In the early 1970s Commonwealth Avenue lost many homes due to eminent domain and the construction of the 210 freeway. The construction area became a dirt playground perfect for playing hide and seek with Kathy Rhoads.

If I ever had a partner in sports, Kathy was it. We competed with each other and with the boys at kickball, tetherball and racing. Many days, Kathy and I would walk to her house through the vacant lot, kicking stones on Foothill Boulevard. We are still friends to this day.

My group of long-term friends get together periodically and have a blast. While I'm with them, I can let my hair down and relax. We get each other because "stuff" happens to them, too, and I have no "splainin'" to do. We compare Lucy stories and laugh until we cry. To me, they are priceless.

Beachfront Vacations with Dad

We camped for vacations, typically at the beach since it was free. My friends loved going with us because my dad was so fun and crazy. With two friends in tow, we would take off in our red VW van, and Dad would blast his classical music with the windows rolled down. Of course, he would rock to the music.

Once we arrived, he would set up camp, followed by the dip in the ocean. After dark, he would throw on his black robe with red Chinese dragons on it. As soon as that happened, my friends would run screaming—my dad's cue to chase them. You can imagine, his arms up like a monster coming at us in the dark...they loved it. What a magical time. Beach camping trips are one of the main memories we reminisce about to this day.

Find Champions Above, Below and In Between

When creating a circle of friends in your work world, look for that same feeling when someone has your back. Quite frankly, you have their back as well. Develop champions at every level in business. A champion is a person who voluntarily takes extraordinary interest in the adoption, implementation, and success of a cause, program, project or product. They care.

"A champion is a person who voluntarily takes extraordinary interest in the adoption, implementation, and success of a cause, program, project or product."

Frank McKenna believed in me before I did. He was the partner who brought me to the dance. In return, I gave 100 percent commitment to the success of the company.

Dance with the partner who brought you to the dance.

When working your way up the ladder, find one or more champions above you in management to help you along the way. Show loyalty, ingenuity, perseverance and dependability. That might sound like a given, but those qualities are hard to find these days. Be the person who grabs the rope and helps pull.

People do business with people they like.

My clients also became champions for me. I was sincere in my desire to give them the best service. If they needed something, all they had to do was pick up the phone and I had their back. But beyond that, we had fun and became good friends.

Here are a few of them:

Steve Barker from Centinela Hospital (of the AK47 story in Los Angeles) brought me with him when he changed hospitals. He brought me major accounts because he trusted me and valued my sincere dedication to finding the win-wins for him.

Diane Bailey started out attending my seminar on Section 125 IRS code 32 years ago when I was still at Corroon. At that time, I would give seminars in hopes of landing clients.

In fact, she ended up walking out because it was so boring. Diane is the godmother of my youngest, Tori. Now, that is a golden friendship.

Joanne Dane accompanied me on several of my escapades. She was a great wing-woman and an even greater Account Executive for my clients. My sweet spot is big-picture strategy and not necessarily execution. Joanne was great at interpreting what I needed in order to put the vision into action. We worked together for eleven years.

Marian Swanson was always smiling at my elevator sna-fus and other Lucy moments, like our night at the 1-star hotel. She was with Caremark. When they made an acquisition, we would often travel together to meet with physicians to talk about their benefits.

In 2008, one of my former employees called to let me know that Marian's husband had passed away. I had retired in 2004. The next day, I flew to Chicago to attend Kevin's funeral. I hung out with her and her family that day. She was such an integral part of my success over our 10 years together, I wanted to be there for her. On those two flights, I wrote my story which became the foundation for this book.

These are just a few of the clients who created my circle of friends. We shared so many laughs and so many heartfelt human moments that I will treasure forever.

Even when starting off on the wrong foot, relationships can be saved and sometimes transformed. First of all, own up to your mistakes. Some of your worst experiences may end up as a springboard for your success. That's what happened with Jim Hillman, Executive Director for Unified Medical Group Association (UMGA).

"Relationships can be saved and sometimes transformed."

Early in my career, I put together a free survey of benefits for each of the Medical Groups. My plan was to share the results with those who participated. Smart idea, right? Well, the snafu happened when I sent a mailing to a list from UMGA.

At the time, I thought it was okay. In my mind, I was offering a service by helping them evaluate their coverages for possible changes. WRONG! I got a call from Jim Hillman, and he proceeded to "rip me another new one" for about ten minutes. When he was finished, I apologized profusely. Once again, I saw my career vanishing before my eyes.

We got past it. In subsequent years, UMGA hired me as a consultant for the annual UMGA Compensation and Benefits Survey, working with Diane Bailey. Jim Hillman became one of my biggest supporters throughout the rest of my career. He included me on his three-day fishing trips down the Rogue river in Oregon where we hosted Medical Group CEO's. I went on seven of those trips. We had some of the best laughs, and I learned a lot from him as a mentor.

Own up to your mistakes. Come up with a solution.

———————————

The same thing happened with Gloria Mayer from Friendly Hills. She started out telling me I should be fired and ended up with us at Lloyd's of London...you just never know what might happen!

People do business with people they like.

———————————

Although the Velvet Glove is sometimes necessary, be very careful before you write off anyone. You never know when that person who is currently a thorn in your side will become your superior or when they will show up again, even after decades, as a decision maker in a major deal you're trying to win.

"Be very careful before you write off anyone."

LEFT: Me, Kathy Rhoads, Cara Badger 1979 CENTER: Cara Bottom left, me 3rd from left middle row RIGHT: Me, Cara and Moody Cabanillas 2014

"Building a golden circle of friends
is a key component of success."

The Allison Heritage:

John Churchill, Duke of Marlborough

I have a common ancestor with John Churchill, known as the 1st Duke of Marlborough. He was a military general who fought many battles for England in the early 1700s. A strategic genius, he was one of the most celebrated generals in European history.

In his largest victory, he led 90,000 soldiers from the front—not from a tent a safe distance away. John Churchill led by example. However, his military prowess comes second, in my opinion, to the respectful way that he treated his soldiers. He took care of them. He had their backs. In return, they were very loyal to him.

"His military prowess comes second to the respectful way that he treated his soldiers."

In my study, I see several similarities between Abraham Lincoln and John Churchill. Both of them inspired loyalty from those above, beneath and in between.

- As an administrator, Churchill's attention to detail meant his troops rarely went short of supplies. His army arrived at their destination intact and fit to fight. His concern for the welfare of the common soldier, his ability to inspire trust and confidence, and his willingness to share the danger of battle earned him admiration from his men. "The known world could not produce a man of more humanity," said Corporal Matthew Bjihop."[82]

This was Churchill's personal brand.

---

[82] D.G. Chandler, "The Old Corporal: Marlborough," *History Today*, Vol. 22 Issue 9, September 1972. https://www.historytoday.com/archive/old-corporal-marlborough

Treat others the way you want to be treated.

- His countenance was mild, thoughtful and commanding. He allowed others to see the real and genuine person that he was.

Be true to you.

- The great success of the Duke was attributed to the Graces, who protected and promoted him. In the hierarchy of English nobility, the Graces are similar to the C-Suite in corporate America. They are closest to the Crown (the CEO). The Graces generally have the ear of the King or Queen. If they like you, you are golden.
- "His manner," Lord Chesterfield declared, "was irresistible, by either man or woman."

People do business with people they like

- "To the "cool head and warm heart" of Marlborough, as King William the Third expressed it, he owed his early and progressive success.
His consideration for others—the gentleness for which he refused what he could not grant—the grace for which he conferred favours—these qualities combined with indefatigable industry, hardihood, and a judgement never prejudiced by passion, were the true sources of Churchill's greatness.[83]

---

[83] A.T., *Memoirs of Sarah Duchess of Marlborough, and of the Court of Queen*

Mentoring Tori

Because I retired before Tori was born, in a sense her siblings paid the price so she could have a stay-at-home mom. With my first two children, I stayed preoccupied with work and traveling, something similar to J.C. This focus on my job allowed me to retire early. Tori has never seen me work outside of the home.

I was room mom for Tori's classes from kindergarten through 5th Grade. I got to know most of the kids in her class and watched friendships develop that have continued to this day. Her 3 or 4 core friends are also good athletes and do well at school. They have each other's backs.

Over the years, Tori has said, "Mom, I have worked hard at having a good circle of friends." Selecting her friends has been a conscious decision.

The same is true for Jamie who wrote an essay that said, "I looked around the playground, and I knew who would get me in trouble and who wouldn't." Both girls made the right choices.

As a parent, I quickly learned how important it is to get to know the parents of your kids' friends. I stay close to the moms of Tori's core friends. We have a lot in common, as they were also athletes in high school. We moms form a close circle around our girls, and we also have each other's backs.

Whether in life or business, building a golden circle of friends is a key component of success.

"Building a golden circle of friends is a key component of success."

A LUCY MOMENT
Crashing the Party

At the height of my career, I was very focused and generally in my own world. I was always in a hurry. On my way to the airport, Joanne Dane and I stopped at the mall. I had a specific item I needed to find and had very little time to find it.

As usual, I was walking fast with Joanne behind me. I rounded a corner and collided with a naked mannequin. The mannequin toppled over just as Joanne reached it. Without missing a beat, she caught the mannequin with a breast in each hand.

Holding on, she got a puzzled expression and said, "So, that's what that feels like."

Cracking up, I grabbed the naked mannequin away from Joanne and set it back in place.

Like I said, Joanne was a great wing-woman.

I was on my way to meet Jim Hillman, Diane Bailey and Mike Suter from Sullivan Kelly. Mike took care of medical malpractice insurance, and I was responsible for working with the Groups for employee benefits.

After we met with the Portland groups, Jim, Diane and Mike decided they are going to stop in Reno on the way home and go snowmobiling. It sounded like fun, so I crashed their party.

At the hotel in Reno, Jim was nice enough to give up his suite for Diane and I. While Diane called home, Jim and I went for a drink downstairs. I took the opportunity to confide in him about deciding whether or not to work with McKenna. I wanted to get his advice and his blessing if I left Corroon. He told me I should be a CEO.

UMGA/Reno: February 1995... from left, Gail DellaVedova CEO, Greater Physicians Medical Group; Mike Suter, Producer, Sullivan Kelly; Diane Bailey, Director of Human Resources/UMGA; Jim Hillman Executive Director/CEO UMGA; John Sherman, Consultant UMGA; and me Senior Consultant, WF Corroon...aka, party crasher!

The next day we rented snowmobiles and had a lot of fun and laughs. Mike Suter rented a limo (those Sullivan Kelly expense accounts were the best!) with a stocked bar. Later, Diane reminded me that she and I stood up through the limo's sunroof on the way back to the hotel. No wonder I loved working with them. That was the best party I've ever crashed, and I was getting paid for it.

Jim Hillman always teased that I should write a book called *Travels with Therese*...better late than never.

CHAPTER 14

Make it Happen

*Make your future dream a present fact, by assuming
the feeling of the wish fulfilled.*[84] ~Wayne Dyer

It was 1974. I was 13 years old. Holding my green bowling ball in front of me, I walked up to the line. Cameras stood in front of me and on the side. Holding the ball up, I stared at the formation of white pins at the end of the alley. For 30 seconds, I held the mental image of the ball hitting just to the right of the pins. Finally, I stepped to the edge and threw.

[84] https://www.goodreads.com/work/quotes/17473999-wishes-fulfilled-mastering-the-art-of-manifesting

As soon as the ball left my hands, I could feel it was a strike. Sure enough, the ball hit just to the right of the pins with that high-pitched crack. The pins scattered.

I had my first strike on a television show called Pinbusters, a bowling game show with kids as contestants. I competed on Pinbusters for the next two shows.

In the fall of 1978, the night before the CIF Championship tennis match against San Marino, I spent most of the evening visualizing placement of the ball and feeling that victory kind of feeling. It was going to be a tough match between two worthy opponents. Both schools were from affluent towns, so many of their players had tennis courts in their backyards and could afford private lessons.

I was from the other side of the Boulevard. I learned to play tennis by hitting the ball against a backboard at Foothill Intermediate School (FIS). Kathy Rhoads's father taught Kathy and I how to play. Five years later, I was in the championship, and it was up to me to be ready. I had to get in the zone. I had to make it happen.

Some might say I was lucky, and maybe I was, but over the years I learned that we make our own luck.

Luck is where preparation meets opportunity.

———————————————

At the beginning, McKenna & Associates grew quickly because they worked in a niche industry. Specializing has its advantages. However, you can also die quickly in a buyout.

Tha's what happened when MedPartners went into a buying frenzy on California medical groups. From Birmingham, Alabama, they had Wall Street backing. When MedPartners acquired Friendly Hills, I may as well just hand over my client list.

I was going to have to upsell my services to their corporate office or kiss my entire book of Medical Groups good-bye. My target: Physician Groups that specialized in managed care.

Malcolm Gladwell defines salesmen as persuaders, charismatic people with powerful negotiation skills. They tend to have an indefinable trait that goes beyond what they say and makes others want to agree with them. They are energetic, enthusiastic, charming and happy. They have the ability to intuitively tune in to the energy and harmony of others. Like my grandfather, this is how I lived and breathed.[85]

I made an appointment with MedPartners Corporate Office in Birmingham. I was a fish out of water as a woman from California trying to do business in the South, but I didn't care. McKenna & Associates had an expertise they wanted and couldn't find anywhere else.

The game was intense, and the stakes were high, but I had been there many times before. Right before we went into the presentation, I visualized their executive signing a Broker of Record letter (the instrument used for a client to assign us their business so that the carriers would recognize us and let us work on their behalf). I felt a conviction in my heart that I was the best person on the planet to deliver the service, and the best person on the planet to make the deal. I was in the zone.

"I felt conviction in my heart."

Don't get me wrong. There weren't any shortcuts. This was the pinnacle of my career. I had used every one of my pearls of wisdom to get to that point.

Two hours later, we left with the signature, as their broker and consultant for all of their acquisitions across the country. I became the partner in charge of managing all lines.

MedPartners was the whale of my career.

---

[85] Malcolm Gladwell, *The Tipping Point: How Little Things Can Make a Big Difference*, (Back Bay Books, January 7, 2002) p 304.

1983 *Italian Scene*

"Dad, you painted this!"

THE ALLISON HERITAGE:

Refuse the No

Pioneers by their very nature make things happen. Certainly, the Allison's were an example of that.

> *The positive thinker sees the invisible, feels the intangible, and achieves the impossible.* ~Winston Churchill

Winston Churchill made it happen. When he became Prime Minister, he wrote in his journal regarding World War II: "At last I had the authority to give directions over the whole scene. I felt as if I were walking with destiny, and that all my past life had been but a preparation for this hour and this trial...."

Churchill brought a naked confidence to his position. He believed in his heart that under his leadership Britain would win the war, even though all indicators said he didn't have a chance.

He refused the no.

Thank God, he didn't listen to naysayers.

Wayne Dyer was another leader who refused the no. Taken from his website: "Despite his childhood spent in orphanages and foster homes, *Dr. Dyer has overcome many obstacles to make his dreams come true...* It is possible for every person to manifest their deepest desires if they honor their inner divinity and constantly choose to live from their "Highest Self.""[86]

During his lifetime, Dr. Wayne Dyer sold more than 100 million books on self-help.

Like Wayne Dyer, my dad overcame many obstacles. He was a survivor. He believed you need to know yourself in order to live from your highest self. Without hardship to overcome, you would never discover yourself.

---

[86] https://www.drwaynedyer.com

Where did I learn this? From my dad, of course! I grew up with my dad making things happen.

My dad painted *Italian Scene* (shown above) in 1983-84 with foresight of what was to come.

In 2003, he, the kids and I went on a Mediterranean Cruise. One morning, Dad and I got up early to view the most beautiful sunrise. As we turned the corner, magnificent Venice unfolded before our eyes...and it looked exactly like the Italian Scene painting. I looked at him and said, "Dad, you painted this!" He just looked at me and smiled.

He made things happen.

The Anatomy of a Connector

Anyone can be a connector. Everything is possible.

"Everything is possible."

From Wayne Dyer, *The Power of Intention*:

Connectors aren't surprised when synchronicity or coincidence brings them the fruits of their intention. They know in their heart that those seemingly miraculous happenings were brought into their immediate life space because they were already connected to them.

To connectors, it all seems simple. Keep your thoughts on what you intend to create. Stay consistently matched up with the field of intention, and then *watch for the clues* that what you are summoning from the all creative Source (in my case, God) is arriving in your life. To a connector, there are simply no accidents. They perceive seemingly insignificant events as being orchestrated in perfect harmony. They believe in synchronicity and aren't surprised when the perfect person for a situation appears, or when someone they've been thinking about calls out of the blue, or when a book arrives unexpectedly in the mail giving them the information they needed, or the money to finance a project mysteriously shows up.[87]

For connectors, it's not about "seeing is believing."

In Wayne Dyer's book *Wishes Fulfilled*, he suggests that if you want to see your dreams come true, then you must, first and foremost, believe they are possible. In other words, the opposite of what you've always believed is true. Seeing isn't believing. Believing is seeing.

You'll see it when you believe it. ~Wayne Dyer

The stories of both "Breath of Life" and "Rhapsody in Blue" came about because of connecting the dots, as my dad would say. When I wrote those two stories, my mind was completely open to exploring the clues that would pop into my mind and figuring out how they were connected.

I knew what the end game was. I knew there was a story. I just needed to put the pieces together. It was as if I had a canvas with the title of the music in the center. The clues allowed me to paint by numbers until the masterpiece was complete, something like my father when he painted *Italian Scene*, then we saw it together in Venice twenty years later. My dad was a connector, too.

"It's like HE gives you clues...not the answer (yet). It's up to you to follow through." "CONNECT THE DOTS...a peace that passes all human understanding...an explosion of spiritual consciousness."

Both "Breath of Life" and "Rhapsody in Blue" are three dimensional with visual performances attached. They came

---

[87] Wayne Dyer, *The Power of Intention*, (Hay House Inc, December 15, 2005), Chapter 15.

together in the realm of possibility. They are two stories that are connected. No accidents…Synchronicity.

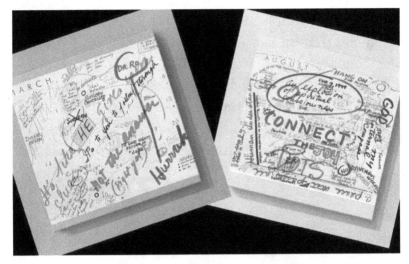

Left: "It's like he gives you clues…but not the answer."
Right: Connect the Dots

This is how things worked during my career. When a goal would come to mind, I never let naysayers deter me. I stayed positive that my goal was going to happen. I would visualize a prospective client signing the letter. When you believe it, you will see it, or as my dad would say, "Do. Act as if it's already been granted."

"Act as if it's already been granted."

As a producer, I used every tool in my tool chest to grow my book of business. Trust me, this can be a powerful key to your success in business, too.

Mentoring Jamie: A Date with Fate

Synchronicity is a state in which you almost feel as if you are in collaborative arrangement with the universe. I felt this in a profound way on August 8, 2002.

In 2002, we were returning to California from Hawaii, and I had a chance to take an upgrade to First Class for one person in our group. I gave it to Jamie. She was eight years old, and she could handle sitting next to a stranger. I thought it would be a treat for her.

After we landed, she came running up to me excited as a child with a new toy. She said, "Mommy, this man gave me a book!"

The book was *Secrets to Success and Inner Peace* by Dr. Wayne Dyer. He wrote a note in the book for her: "Jamie, To the nicest girl I ever flew with from Maui. Wayne Dyer. 8 Aug 02."

My text to Jamie on September 1, 2015:

Me: Wayne Dyer passed away. You sat next to him when you were 8 coming back from Hawaii. It's an article about his philosophy.

Jamie: I remember that...he gave me a book with a note.

Me: Read article

Jamie: Heading to class and I can't get my email to refresh. I will later.

Me: Pretty special that you got to sit next to him.

Thirteen years later, I followed the clues and found a harmonious string of events. In "Breath of Life" from *Snow White and the Huntsman*, I first connected the music with the title. My dad took his first breath of life on that date. Jamie was connected through her synchronized skating and the music (Jamie looks like Snow White in the video). My grandmother's last name was Snow, and she took her last Breath of Life two floors down from my dad in the same hospital. No accidents. Synchronicity.

"They (connectors) perceive seemingly insignificant events as being orchestrated in perfect harmony."[88]

"Rhapsody in Blue" also had a string of clues. My dad had profound connections. Doors would open up for him. He sat by my neighbor in a church of 12,000 people. "Rhapsody in Blue" was his favorite music, and Jamie's team wore blue. Dad wrote a love note about music.

Jamie sat next to Wayne Dyer on a flight from Maui in 2002, then Jamie skated in the World Championships in 2015. That was not an accident. When I made that decision to send Jamie to First Class, I had four other options. I didn't sit next to Wayne Dyer. My dad didn't sit next to him. I didn't have my nephew Justin sit next to him. I did not send Michael to sit next to him. I "randomly" sent my eight-year-old daughter to sit next to Wayne Dyer. Why?

Because she would become a synchronized skater on the World stage.

It is every skater's dream. This little-known sport shows the true essence of synchronicity and that is a cornerstone of Dr. Dyer's manifestation teachings.

---

[88] Wayne Dyer, *The Power of Intention*, (Hay House Inc, December 15, 2005), Chapter 15.

Nothing is more beautiful and powerful than watching sixteen women on the ice, skating in perfect harmony...skating as one.

No accidents. Synchronicity.

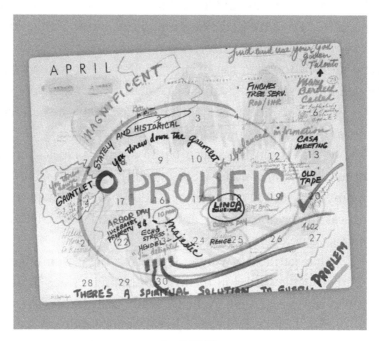

April 2002

Dr. Wayne Dyer – "There is a spiritual solution to every problem."

As I was writing this book, the thought occurred to me that I should look at my dad's 2002 calendar again for any clues (just like I knew I needed to look at Lotta's diary). So, I flipped through his 2002 calendar to see if something popped up. Sure enough, something did. In April before our Hawaii trip in August, Dad wrote on his calendar, "Dr. Wayne Dyer, There's a Spiritual Solution to Every Problem," the title of one of Wayne Dyer's books.

Four months later, we flew home on the same plane with him, and Jamie sat next to him in First Class.

My dad and Wayne Dyer had similar beliefs, with one exception: my dad wrote down what he prayed about. He manifested answers to his prayers through pads, calendars and paintings. I'm sure that for many hours on the plane, Jamie talked Dr. Dyer's ear off about skating!

On that plane that day were two of the most self-actualized, spiritual men I've ever known about: my dad and Wayne Dyer. Both had manifested dreams and received answers to prayers. That day, they crossed paths. There are no accidents. There are no coincidences. There is only synchronicity.

LEFT: Jamie and coach Laura CENTER: Wayne Dyer
RIGHT: My dad and I circa 1970.

We got off the plane—a father and daughter with a profound connection, a man who taught the world how to manifest dreams, and a little girl that loved figure skating—not realizing that 13 years later, there would be a date with fate. There would be "Rhapsody in Blue."

 Dwell in possibility. ~Emily Dickenson

A LUCY MOMENT
Monte Carlo and Scotch Tape

In the mid-1990s I won a trip for two to attend the Monte Carlo Grand Prix in the South of France. I took Joanne Dane who had worked for me for years.

The plan was that we would stay in Nice for the first couple of nights. In the mid '90s, the French did not like it if visitors couldn't speak their language. When we arrived at the hotel, something had happened with the reservation. They did not have it. They told us they had no room available. I almost cried that *I Love Lucy* kind of cry because we were so tired from the trip.

The hotel staff finally came up with something. The bellman took us to our room. It was tiny, but beggars can't be choosers. I barely got any sleep that night because the room had so much flea powder, we almost choked. They had put us in the maid quarters.

The next morning, I called my office and asked them to get us out of there. As a result, we ended up in the beautiful town of Eze in an old castle called the Chateau de La Chevre d'Or (The Castle of the Golden Goat). It had the most beautiful view of Monte Carlo as well as a cascading view down to the Mediterranean Sea.

After that awful night in Nice, I thought things had definitely turned for the better. The next night, we had an invitation to go to dinner with Albert, Prince of Monaco which he hosted for the Grand Prix. I had a beautiful long, black gown for the special occasion.

When I took it out of my suitcase and held it up to me, the hem dragged the ground by 2 or 3 inches. Not to worry. I called the front desk for some scotch tape. Joanne and I proceeded to tape the hem. Problem solved.

The road to Monte Carlo was one bend after another. After 30 minutes, the driver let us off in front of the Yacht Club. Prince Albert and a guest were walking up the steps with another couple. We walked up the steps behind them. With every step, my hem started coming undone. Scotch tape dragged behind me.

Joanne followed me, holding up my hem (classic Lucy and Ethel). I kept walking, thinking, She's got this. When we got inside, not only do we not speak French, but we are two American women with no men, no diamonds and a taped hem. At the guest check-in, they clearly believed we were gate crashing. Noticeably surprised when we showed them our invitation, they were in no hurry to help us.

Joanne went into the bathroom, and I waited outside. A familiar-looking guy was waiting as well. I moved closer for a better look. It was Hugh Grant, the British actor. I saw him in *Four Weddings and a Funeral, Notting Hill* (one of my favorites), *Bridget Jones Diary* and *Love Actually* to name a few. My tape snafu not only happened with Prince Albert but Hugh Grant and his date.

Meanwhile, Joanne was in line for the bathroom. The woman in front of her leaned her arm on the wall, displaying a solid diamond cuff. It was Elizabeth Hurley, British actress and model. Hugh Grant and Elizabeth Hurley had a high-profile relationship. They were the focus of much attention in British and International media in those days.

We got through the dinner without any more mishaps. When we were leaving, we walked outside to look for a taxi.

Unfortunately, at this time of night all the taxis were already taken. No one was eager to help.

To make matters worse, I was used to having Jerry Sullivan's driver in London. Spoiled, yes. God forbid, I'd have to get my own car.

Finally, I got hold of an English speaker at the hotel, and they said they would send a car. While we were waiting, it started to rain. With no place to hide, all we could do was endure. My black gown was a disaster in more ways than one.

The next day, Joanne and I decided to go sunbathing on a private beach by the Yacht Club. In the French Riviera, women sunbathe topless. If you don't, you look odd. Besides, who's going to know us anyways? When in Rome…

The European men could care less. The American men, on the other hand, had sunglasses on to hide their staring.

About 30 minutes into our sunbathing, Joanne takes a full-on dive for her top.

"What are you doing?" I asked.

Joanne: "There's John!"

"Who's John?"

Joanne: "John with the wooden leg!"

I looked and, sure enough, there stood a man with shorts on and a wooden leg. "How do you know John?"

Joanne: "He plays cards at the club with my dad back home!"

We put our clothes on and went over to say hi. Meanwhile, I'm sizin' him up thinking, *Did he see her or didn't he?*

Imagine the next card game back home. "So, John said he saw Joanne in Monaco, and when I say saw, I really mean saw…"

If Lucy and Ethel ran into British royalty and Hollywood icons in Europe, this would definitely be their story!

CHAPTER 15

Expect Miracles

Prayer sets up good vibrations "to—receive."
~Gould Allison

The doctor said, "He has a matter of months...."

He continued talking, but his voice became meaningless background noise.

"...a matter of months to live..." echoed in my head as though he had shouted it into a desert canyon.

The year was 1998. My dad had been in the hospital many times before, but this was the first time a doctor had given him a final date. When I took Dad home that day, I packed him up to come live with me for his remaining months. Once there, I put on his favorite music for him as he looked out at the water.

Dad had his first quadruple bypass at age 57. He had a second quadruple bypass 27 years later, multiple angioplasties, ablation procedures, a failed stent, and at the end he took 24 medications. He had countless ER trips where I thought this was the end. Like a cat with nine lives, he would rally back.

After the doctor's dire prediction in 1998, Dad lived seventeen more years.

My dad, Gould Allison, was an extraordinary human being. His connection to others and his relationship with God were like nothing else I have ever seen. Doors would open up, and people would come into his life in answer to his prayers. He was living proof that all things are possible with God's help.

His prayers ranged from asking for inspiration for a painting, to requesting an attitude adjustment, healing his back, or just to get through the latest medical challenge. When he wrote his prayers down, they were answered.

His life from 1999 on was a miracle.

A 1999 article in the *Los Angeles Times* said:

...and now the longtime La Canada Flintridge resident lay in a hospital bed, slowly drowning in his own fluids due to heart failure...It was devastating news when the doctor told Allison's adult children that their father would likely lose his life within a matter of months..."

But death's grasp lost hold of Allison as he was touched by an angel of revival. "God wanted me to live... I can't figure it out."[89]

---

[89] "LIFE AS ART, Loss of a loved one and a brush with death give local painter Gould Allison's life – and art – special meaning," (*Los Angeles*

An abstract impressionist painter, Allison creates his works on a back patio, inside his garage, and puts his finishing touches after hanging his creations on a wooden fence.

Tragedy has found Allison several times in his life... "I'm used to tragedies," he said. "So, when the blessings come, I'm grateful. I'm very grateful for what I have. I'm especially grateful for every day."

"God has carried me without me knowing it. God is inside me. I can feel the presence beyond myself... I've been given the chance through the grace of God to be who I am."[90]

Here are some of his written prayers:

Prayer Pad #2 – "Good Stuff for Positive"

September 21, 2001

Dear Jesus – Oh, how wonderful you are. You have taken us through many crises in the past and I can see you work in these days. Thank you! I know that you will bring this country thru its darkest hour as you have in the past. Thank you...

Prayer Pad #3 – "Evidence of God"

September 25, 2001

Dear Jesus – The blessings continue and I am so grateful. Thank you, thank you, thank you. I write these prayers KNOWING that they are already answered. Just in the last two days some have been answered re: my show...I know that all things are possible as you Promise.

Times, October 29, 1999).

[90] Ibid.

Prayer Pad #22 – "Writing is the highest form of prayer – To me"

I know why he lived so long. With God all things are possible.

My dad also had an all-time love of music. Whenever I took him to the ER, if we arrived at the hospital without his headphones, that was the emergency. His health came second.

After he passed, I found these pages in one of his journals.

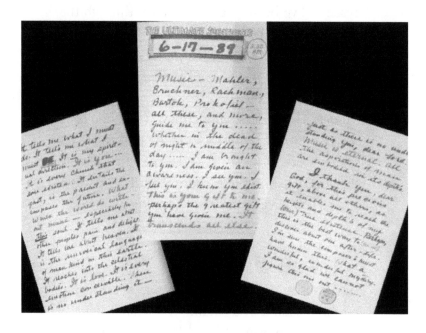

A Love Note

In August 1989, Dad woke up in the middle of the night to write, what I call a Love Note. It is filled with love and all about music, the same as he was:

Music – Mahler, Rachmaninoff, Bruckner, Bartok, Prokofiev – all these, and more, guide me to you....whether in the dead of night or middle of the day.... I am brought to you. I am given awareness. I see you. I feel you. I know you exist. This is your gift to me. Perhaps the greatest gift you have given me. It transcends all else.

It tells me what I must do. It tells me what I must BE. It is my spiritual direction. It is you... It is every church that ever existed. It entails the past, is the present, and encompasses the future. What would the world be without music— especially for this soul.

It tells me about other people's pain and delight. It tells me about heaven. It is the universal language of mankind on this earth. It reaches into the celestial body. It is love. It is every emotion conceivable. There is no understanding it—just as there is no understanding you, dear Lord. Music is eternal. All of the aspirations of man are embodied in its depths.

I thank you dear God for this precious gift, above all others, as it enables me to reach the height and depth of my (our) true existence. Perhaps this is the best way to discover our afterlife. I'm sure the composers must have known

this. What a wonderful, wonderful mystery. I am
so glad that we cannot figure this one out.

A composer and pianist of popular and classical music in
the early 20th century, George Gershwin was my dad's favorite.
In 1955, Leonard Bernstein said of George Gershwin: "The
Rhapsody (in Blue) is not a composition at all. It's a string of
separate paragraphs stuck together into one piece. The themes
are terrific, inspired, God-given. I don't think there has been
such an inspired melodist on this earth since Tchaikovsky."[91]

"Rhapsody in Blue" combines my Dad's two favorite
types of music—jazz rhythm and classical.

Life As Art

Like the composer of a symphony, my dad would lay the
foundation for his calendar art by building the story. Using an
Ansel Adams calendar (1992-2009), he would document his
personal life and all current events on most of the days. Next, he
used colored markers to build a crescendo of emotion for that
month. Whether it was a conversation, a visit, a birth, the passing of a pet, a current event—everything was there. Periodically,
he would punctuate his calendar symphony with a painting on
canvas.

Anyone who had an interaction with him during the year
would find their name and, most likely, his thoughts forever
engraved in his calendar.

My dad used his calendars and prayer pads to show that
when he prayed, his prayers were answered. He left sixty yellow
prayer pads filled with written prayers and their answers.

Touched by an Angel

Della Reese created a show called "Touched by an Angel"
which aired from 1994-2003. After my dad's 1998 resurgence in

---

[91] "Why Don't You Run Upstairs and Write a Nice Gershwin Tune?"
Leonard Bernstein, *Atlantic Monthly*, April 1955.

health, he started worshipping in the Beverly Hills church pastored by Della herself. He was the only white guy in the congregation, wearing one of his signature red Hawaiian shirts and dancing with joyous abandon. Della and her husband, Rev. Williams, loved him. They'd smile and say, "He'll dance at the least provocation."

2004 GOD COMES THROUGH – Dear God – Please heal my back –
Thank you God, NO Surgery

LEFT: Della Reese RIGHT: My dad

On one of his calendars, Dad wrote that Rev. Williams had called him. He said that my dad was "unrepeatable, one of a kind." Oh, and guess how long they talked. You guessed it, 45 minutes.

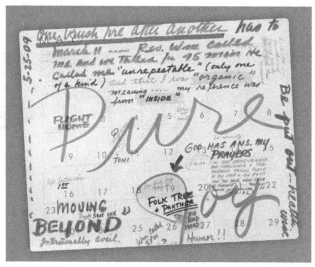

"Rev. Wm called me and we talked for 45 minutes…
GOD HAS ANSWERED MY PRAYERS"

He wrote his prayers in red during this period of zeal:

"I have so much to look forward to this summer."

"Thanks Jesus. My heart is full as I EMBARK on all of this with ZEAL."

"One must remember that God is shy—all we have to do is say YES."

"Most often—the easiest things are the hardest."

It was amazing to me how my dad went through so many tragedies and yet still managed to be positive throughout his life. He was a gift to all who knew him. My dad had a grateful heart. As a result, he was a magnet for miracles.

"My dad had a grateful heart and as a result, he was a magnet for miracles."

Frame Jamie

Following my dad's footsteps, I also saw miracles.

Shortly after Jamie was born, she contracted Respiratory Syncytial Virus (RSV), a virus that produces a lot of mucous. I thought she had a cold, so I took her to the pediatrician. As I was in the waiting room, Jamie coughed and choked. Her lips turned purple. After several intense moments, the doctor told me to take Jamie to the hospital, where she remained in an oxygen tent for eight days.

After I returned to work from maternity leave, I realized that I had missed a 5500 deadline for a very big client. One of the most terrifying deadlines to miss is with the IRS. I panicked as this form had hefty penalties.

Against all odds, I put together a long letter explaining that it was my fault because of extenuating circumstances with the birth of my daughter. I went into what happened and that she was hospitalized for eight days and that they shouldn't penalize my client.

I received a letter back from them stating that the form could be filed late, without penalties. It was a miracle. The IRS had a heart! I named that letter the "Frame Jamie" letter. In fact, I framed it and put it on the wall!

Take the ethical road because it is the right thing to do, and you might just end up with a miracle.

Always take the high road.

———————————————

1999-2003 POSSIBLE

"My dad had a greatful heart.
As a result he was a magnet
for miracles."

Rhapsody in Blue

I walked with him through the last seventeen years of his life, seeing firsthand how he lived. While we have an extraordinary heritage, my dad has always been the gem.

My next-door neighbor, Marilyn Giordano Grangruth, had seen Dad at my house a few times, but she had never formally met him. Here's what Marilyn told me:

> We go to a massive church with four services with over 12,000 people. My husband and I never sit in the balcony, but this one time we did. A couple wanted to move into our row, so I told Wes to move down and let them have our seats. I did a double take, and there stood Gould! I could not believe the timing and seat change. It was meant to be.

Early in April, 2014, Dad had a bad episode of congestive heart failure and went on bed rest. Instead of hiring someone from a service to prepare his meals and stay with him, I paid Jamie to take care of her grandfather. My dad would talk her ear off while music played in the background, and Jamie cooked for him or brought his medicine. It was a miracle summer for both of them.

After my dad passed, I sent the family a text asking which songs reminded them of their grandpa, so I could include those songs in the video of his life. One grandchild sent, "What a Wonderful World." Jamie sent "Rhapsody in Blue."

One of my cousins sent a note that said,

> Now that he is pure angel, he is free to broadcast his amazing being from the heavens. When I feel

light and hope, I know he is a part of it. When facing trial and despair, mine or others, his many examples of finding the joy and love in life is always a beacon. Such a dear loved cherished man.

He and I had talked about holding his celebration at his condo. A few days after he passed, I came up with the idea of an art show. We had the celebration of my dad's life on Saturday, April 4, 2015. I set his condo up like an art exhibit with his paintings all labeled on easels. His calendars lay on a table. It was a beautiful, small event with family and close friends. I acted as the docent.

LEFT: Jamie's text April 1, 2015 " RIGHT: My dad and I in 2013

Jann Buaiz attended the celebration. A couple of years earlier, Jann's husband, George, had died suddenly. We were all devastated. At the time, I didn't know Jann very well, but I felt compelled to go and sit with her all day.

That evening at my dad's celebration, Jann gave me a silver chime in the shape of a heart in a red velvet pouch. My dad's favorite color was red. The card said: "When you hold it and swirl it, pay attention to what you see and hear…spiritual attraction." Every time it chimed, it reminded me of my dad.

The next Saturday, Jamie was scheduled to compete in the World Synchronized Skating Championships in Canada. I had to switch gears from sadness about my dad to happiness for Jamie. This was her first of two back-to-back World Championships.

Before Tori and I took off for the competition, I dropped the red bag with the silver heart into my purse. The heart chimed a lot that trip. Dad was a talker!

My dad and I had been through the trenches together. We were so close. For years before he passed away, I did a lot of pre-grieving. In 2008 when his health was failing, I said to him, "It's not fair. You will go before me, and I will be left behind."

He pointed to my heart and said matter-of-fact without hesitation, "Oh, but my spirit will be in you."

And it was.

"Music…It is you…It is every Church that ever existed…It tells me about heaven…it is the universal language of mankind on this earth…It is love."

Mentoring Jamie:
The World Championships, Canada 2015

If you are an elite skater, it is almost impossible to make it to the U.S. Championships, so skaters often switch to synchronized skating. The U.S. sends forty elite skaters to the World Championships each year. Just like the Olympics, competitors had a short program night and a free skate night. The two scores combined determine the final placement. Synchronized skating has not been sanctioned into the Olympics, so the World Championships are like the Olympics.

The World Championships include 25 teams from 20 countries because 5 powerhouse countries send two teams: USA, Russia, Canada, Sweden and Finland.

In 2015, after the short program, fierce competition began for the 6-10 spots. USA 1 had been pushed out of the top five by Finland 2 with Canada 2 on their tail. That meant Jamie's team, USA 2 (known as Miami University) might not make tenth place.

Team USA 2 skated their short program to "The World is Ours" by Aloe Blacc X and David Correy:

Run like your born to fly...

Live like you'll never die...

Dare what you dare to dream...

The world is ours, light up the world, light up the world...

The same song was featured at the 2014 World Cup in Brazil. Michael was in the stands watching that year.

The second night of competition, the entire arena felt electrified. Everything, and I mean everything for these ladies, was on the line. The order of skate goes from worst score to best score from the night before. USA 1 was at a disadvantage as they were slotted to skate with the 6-10 teams. This meant the judges were not going to score them as high as if they were 1-5.

USA 2 was happy because they were in 9th position going into the Free Skate with a score of 54.73. Sweden 2 was in 8th ahead of us with 59.12, and Russia 2 was breathing down our neck in 10th position with a score of 54.69. The play: go after Sweden 2 and become 8th in the world.

Russia 2 skated a beautiful program for a score of 115.77.

To watch Russia 2 skate their free skate, go to YouTube:
2015 WSSC Hamilton - Tartastan - Russia 2 - Free Skating
https://www.youtube.com/watch?v=Z65mUPlFEEw&t=82s

When USA 2 reached the ice, the crowd erupted into applause. This was it. This was what Jamie had been working toward since she was four years old. She made her dream of skating on the World Stage come true.

Jamie has the undeniable conquering spirit of a pioneer. For me, I wanted to beat the boys on the playground and in business. For Jamie, she excelled in her sport and in her education, always pushing her limits.

USA 2 started out strong with lifts in the first two minutes. The crowd clapped to the Elvis medley. The girls were smiling and are having the time of their lives. Their elements were great. Their facial expressions were awesome. Toward the end, the team backed into each other. They intersected when Elvis said, "blue suede shoes." They were on fire, and the crowd went wild.

Picture from figure skating magazine. Jamie is middle right.

Once they finished, they received a standing ovation. Parents were crying, yelling and waving.

To watch USA 2 skate their free skate, go to YouTube:
2015 World Synchro Champs FS Team USA 2
https://www.youtube.com/watch?v=2HS6ppadtJ4&t=37s

Music: Viva Elvis
The girls went to the kiss-and-cry area to wait for their scores. Meanwhile, the Jumbotron was showing highlights from their skate. Five minutes later, the French-Canadian announcer said, "Team United States of America 2 has a score of 117.06." Their best score of the season, they had edged out Russia 2 by two points. Now the performance of Sweden 2 would determine who would take 8th place.

Playing for Keeps

Sweden 2 started out as graceful ballerinas poised for a rendition of Swan Lake. About a minute into their performance, they had a fallen swan. One of their lifts did not go up. My dad must have been doing some Tonya Harding moves from heaven because that just doesn't happen at this level of competition. Sweden 2 lost their composure and ended up in 11th place. USA 1 placed 7th and USA 2 placed 8th.

To watch Sweden 2 skate their Free Skate, go to YouTube:
2015 WSSC Hamilton - Boomerang - Sweden 2 - Free Skating
https://www.youtube.com/watch?v=5Vsi3_XpXA4

The top 5 still had to perform. Canada 1 (known as Nexxice) went first and scored 71.06. Finland 1 placed 2nd with 70.39. Finland 1 skated flawlessly and came in with a score of 143.67.

When Canada 1 took the ice, the audience came to their feet to welcome them, waving Canadian flags. They have fifteen women and one guy, all dressed in black velvet.

I had never seen Canada 1's long program before that evening. It was surreal. I was sitting at my daughter's World Championships when my dad's celebration of life was exactly one week before. Canada 1's music started. Sixteen skaters moved in unison. They were dressed in black (ebony) with white skates (ivory) as the keys.

The guy broke out as the composer. He was George Gershwin, and they are skating to "Rhapsody in Blue." As their performance unfolded, I saw them performing the thoughts from Dad's Love Note.

"Music is eternal"
No accidents. There is only synchronicity.
I had heard the piece so many times, but this time it was more than the music.
"It is the universal language of mankind on this earth."
I felt like I was watching the performance of my dad's life, except this time he was Gershwin and the skaters were performing a rendition of his life on a sheet of ice, where I had spent countless hours with him and his grandchildren.

It was only fitting that the performance of his life included him and fifteen women. He had so many friends who were women. Not in a romantic sense, but in the deep unconditional acceptance of true friendship. To many, he was like a father. He had 3 daughters, 2 granddaughters, 7 nieces, countless women activist friends, Cara...and at the end, 4 caregivers who loved him. We called them his four angels.
The masterpiece on the ice went on...

"I am given awareness."
The music started out slow as they stretched their arms from a long night's sleep, and then gradually sped up with dramatic twists and turns, in groups of 4—Dad with his 3 daughters.
They held hands and glided into one circle.

"I am brought to you."
The composer effortlessly intersected with the other skaters and 16 became as 1.

"It is Love. It is every emotion conceivable."
He took his mother's hand to dance and then lost her in the dissonance of the music.

"It entails the past, is the present, and encompasses the future."
With strength and resolve, Dad lifted himself up so many times—through the death of my sister, his mother, his brother—and he lifted our family. He took care of us when he lost his job. He was our foundation. As I sat there watching the performance, I realized that it wasn't only my family he lifted. It was me. He had always been my rock.

"What would the world be without music—
especially for this soul."
All the while, my dad stayed in harmony with all the skaters coming in and out of his life.
They glided across the ice in a perfect square.

"It tells me about heaven."
I felt like I was back in our den in La Canada. He was painting while I skipped around the house.

"I feel you. I know you exist."
I could see the red van with him swaying to the music.

"It is every church that ever existed."
I saw him in his rocking chair moving with the music.
I saw him looking out at the water in my backyard with the music.

"It reaches into the celestial body."
His arms shot up with each crash of the cymbals, like they did when he was splashing a new color on the canvas.

"It transcends all else."
I felt like I had gone through a lifetime to watch his lifetime in these moments.

"I thank you dear God for this precious gift."
The feelings were so familiar. My dad and I had been in sync all along.

"Perhaps this is the best way to discover our after-life. I'm sure the composers must have known this. "
Near the end, my dad and another skater glided effortlessly in and out of the other skaters, and I realized that she was me as I helped him to the finish line.
He bowed to loud applause.
The masterpiece of his life was complete.
I whispered the words,

"This is your gift for me. Perhaps the greatest gift you have given me."
He had a Gold Medal finish.

To watch Canada 1 skate for the Gold go to YouTube:
2015 WSSC Hamilton - Nexxice - Canada 1 - Free Skating
https://www.youtube.com/watch?v=M7kHhy9A0Ns&t=340s

Music: "Rhapsody in Blue" by George Gershwin

A LUCY MOMENT
April Fools

After my dad passed away, I asked the family to send me stories about him. This one came from my cousin Gwyn whose father was my Dad's brother, Ned.

It was April Fool's Day and Uncle Gould was staying for an extended visit. Mom found it the perfect opportunity to take advantage of their mutual sense of humor.

Uncle Gould loved his coffee, so that morning she substituted the freeze-dried instant coffee with freeze dried instant cocoa and the sugar with salt. We all waited for him to wake up and do the first thing he did every morning, make a cup of coffee.

Finally, he came to the kitchen and made himself a cup of coffee with the altered ingredients. We all went to sit down with him at the dining room table, and he began to talk and talk...and talk. When he paused for a moment, he would lift the cup to his lips, but just before he took a sip, he would continue talking. The cup would go back down to the table until the next pause.

Then up the cup would go to his lips... but no. At the last minute, he would resume his story and the cup would go down.

Every time he looked like he was about to taste his coffee, my Mom, my sisters and I would watch the cup go up and hold our breath in anticipation…then down it would go.

This went on for so long that Uncle Gould finally said, "This coffee will be cold by now, I will make a fresh cup and be right back." He did and the whole thing started again. Up the cup would go to his lips, then he would continue talking and down it would go again without tasting it.

"Finally, he said, "I had better drink this one before it gets cold." At that point he took a sip and burst into laughter. "I get it" he said. "April Fools!" we cheered.

Of course, he got it. Uncle Gould was clever, intelligent, interesting, engaging and had the best sense of humor I have ever encountered in anyone. Listening to him was one of life's great pleasures.

I really wasn't kidding about the 45-minute rule!

CHAPTER 16

The Turning Point

While we try to teach our children all about life, our children teach us what life is all about.[92] ~Angela Schwindt

Two months after my dad's passing, Michael said casually over breakfast, "Mom, I'm moving to New York."

My heart dropped. I gave him that look of, *Really?*

---

[92] https://www.passiton.com/inspirational-quotes/7574-while-we-try-to-teach-our-children-all-about

Trying to sound calm, I picked up my toast. "Are you sure you want to go to New York?" I held my breath, waiting for his answer.

"Yes, I want to experience what it's like to live outside of Southern California. Something about New York draws me. I want my chance to make it there.

"When?"

"The beginning of September."

That was the full conversation.

He's definitely my son. When we make up our minds, discussions are done. We go.

Michael is a fifth-generation Californian, a rare breed. He's an adventurous pioneer with that undeniable conquering spirit. By choosing New York, he was going full circle, not only with our heritage, but to the exact place that caused me to make the tough decision to leave the business.

I'm not going to lie. I was beyond upset about his leaving. The two most important men in my life, my father and my son, were leaving six months apart. But this wasn't about me.

Michael moved at the beginning of September and started his new position on my dad's birthday, September 8, 2015. He was going to be fine. My dad was looking out for him.

The afternoon I finished writing the "Breath of Life" vignette about my dad and my grandmother, Lotta Snow. Michael texted me a picture of the view from his office window. Standing tall in the photo was the One World Trade Center—the building that replaced the Twin Towers, now the tallest building in the United States.

Instantly, that photo took me back fourteen years.

At the height of my career, I loved to visit New York City. During the holidays, I loved the lights and Christmas decorations. Sometimes, I made plans to meet with our reinsurers around the Fourth of July, so I could watch the fireworks over the Statue of Liberty from a boat on the Hudson River.

Those visits gave me a chance to shop and visit the restaurants as well as see the sights. Sometimes I took my sister, and we'd have a fabulous time. From that vantagepoint in my life, I always figured I had another twenty years in the game. The view from the top was fabulous.

One day, a little after seven in the morning my dad called my house. "Turn on the news," he said.

"Why?"

"Just turn on the news." He hung up without saying more. Odd.

I went downstairs where my eight-year-old daughter, Jamie, was eating cereal. I turned on my television. One of the Twin Towers was in flames. Wondering if this were a movie, I watched a plane crash, in slow motion, into the second tower. Our AON offices were in the South Tower. This couldn't be real.

But it was.

The view from Windows on the World

I had only been in the Twin Towers twice before to go to the Windows on the World restaurant on the 107th floor of the North Tower. Once in 1998, I had invited my sister, Cheri, to come with me to New York, so we could celebrate her fortieth birthday. The main event for us was dinner at the famous restaurant. It had one of the most spectacular views in the world, and we were in time to see the sunset. That memory would remain forever seared into my mind.

Windows on the World was the site of the "Falling Man" photo. Two hundred people made the decision to jump that day.[93]

Watching the news, I calculated New York time, and it was around 10 a.m. I could imagine those poor people arriving for work as usual, meeting at the coffee station with morning chit-chat and settling into their desks. They had no idea what was about to happen.

While you never know what you will do in time of crisis, I know two things about myself. I am programmed to help people, and I am a rule follower. If the Port Authority told us to stay, I would have stayed.

"The building is secure. The safest place is inside; stay
calm and do not leave."[94]

The plane hit the South Tower at the 77th floor. AON occupied floors above 93.

While I was watching the live news report, people inside the building were calling family members.

"They said the building is secure, don't evacuate...we
saw an explosion ball, something was coming at us"

---

[93] Tom Junod, "The Falling Man" *Esquire*, September 9, 2016.

[94] Anger of survivors told to stay inside blazing towers – Ed Vulliamy, New York, September 16, 2001.

"Tell my dad, that I love him very much. And make sure you tell my mom that I love her..." ~AON employee, Gregory Milanowycz who perished that day.

The Twin Towers

"We need to get some air...why did I listen to them... we're overlooking the Financial Center...there's three of us, two broken windows...Oh God! Oh..." ~AON Vice President Kevin Cosgrove, who was lost in the building collapse.

Watching the buildings collapse, I lost my breath and started sobbing. I had a plane ticket in my purse from LAX to JFK for the next day. My appointment was with AON on the 98th floor of the South Tower on September 13, 2001.

Jamie asked, "Mommy, why are you crying?"

"Two days from today, I am scheduled to be in a meeting in that second tower."

She said, "Mommy, if you were in that tower, I would fly a plane across the country and come get you out!"

AON lost 176 people that morning, including Wendy Faulkner, an AON vice president who was in New York on the 104th floor of the South Tower for a meeting.[95] Her daughter was the same age as my Michael.

That day changed our nation and the world. It also changed my perspective on my life and my role in business. It is easy to forget who you are doing it for, and I had a massive wake up call.

After 9/11, I wanted to stay close to home. One afternoon, I was playing garage hockey with Michael, age 11, and it struck me that my children needed me close. I could stay in the business and make millions more, but why? As my dad would say, "Just because you can, doesn't mean you should."

"I could stay in the business and make millions more, but why?"

My father grew up without his parents. The family wealth went away, too. I was not going to risk that happening to my kids. I was not going to let that part of our history repeat itself.

Playing garage hockey with my son, I made the decision to retire as soon as I could. The best gift I could give Michael and

---

[95] Stevenson Swanson, "For AON Corp. It Has Been A Struggle to Move On," *Chicago Tribune*, March 11, 2002.

Jamie was my time. Nothing was more important than the footprint I would leave with them.

I also knew that playing for keeps includes knowing when to cash in your Monopoly money and go home.

"I also knew that playing for keeps includes knowing when to cash in your Monopoly money and go home."

I retired in 2004 to stay at home with my kids. I walked away and never looked back. Because I did, I also took care of my dad the last eleven years of his life. He often spoke about how glad he was that I had chosen to stay at home with my children. I could hear in his voice how he related that to his own loss when he was a child.

"I walked away and never looked back."

9/11 has affected each of my kids differently. Even though Tori wasn't born yet, 9/11 still affected her. She posted her feelings about it on September 11, 2019. From the mouths of babes....

LEFT: Tori's post in 2019 RIGHT: Michael's view from his office in 2015…One World Trade Center in the distance.

"On this day my mom was supposed to be in this building, if she was and did not survive, I would have never been born. Things happen for a reason."

In 2016, Jamie went on spring break to New York. I received a phone call from her, and she was crying. She had gone into the room with all of the pictures of those who perished. The reality of how close I came to being in the building affected her deeply.

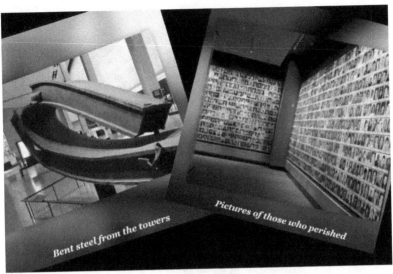

LEFT: Bent steal from the tower RIGHT: Room with pictures
of those who perished

She said, "Your picture could have been there."

"I know," I said and cried with her.

Like Tori said, everything happens for a reason.

Looking back, I'm grateful for every opportunity, for every relationship, for every win and every Lucy Moment. Those eighteen years were filled with hard work and excitement. They were strenuous and demanding and a little magical.

Everyone always said I had a guardian angel. Deep inside, I know it's true.

2018 Huntington Beach Tori, Michael, me, Jamie

About the Author

Therese Allison started her career in the insurance brokerage field in 1987. In the 1990s she became a partner in McKenna & Associates, a firm with close ties to Lloyd's of London. AON Corporation bought McKenna & Associates in 1998. Therese became an Executive Vice President for AON's National Healthcare Practice. She received a Bachelor's Degree from California Polytechnic State University, San Luis Obispo. In 2004, Therese retired to stay home with her three children. She currently lives in Huntington Beach, California.

Email contact: allisonpfk3@gmail.com

Visit her web site at
www.PlayingForKeeps21.org
to view these images in full color.

Chapter Calendar image Reference List

Chapter 1:   1996: Partnership for Therese

Chapter 2:   1995: Gag Order Therese - Therese Landed PPS

Chapter 3:   1995: ALLISON AVE.

Chapter 4:   1995: Mullikin landed by T...J.C. Allison

Chapter 5:   2006: Gigi's GIFT

Chapter 6:   1995: Cultivate the Emergent

Chapter 7:   1995: First outline for ALLISON Book

Chapter 8:   1994: JAMIE ALLISON CARDER a year of possibility

Chapter 9:   1997: Therese London

Chapter 10:   1992: JAPAN TRADE

Chapter 11:   1992: "I am buying the election.....because the American people can't afford to."

Chapter 12: 2004: Abraham Lincoln

Chapter 13:   1995: THERESE PORTLAND OREGON

Chapter 14:   2002: DO...Act as though it has already been granted

Chapter 15:   1998: WITH GOD ALL THINGS ARE POSSIBLE GEORGE GERSHWIN'S 100TH

Chapter 16:   2001: ATTACK!